Composition Studies Through a Feminist Lens

LENSES ON COMPOSITION STUDIES
Series Editors, Sheryl I. Fontaine and Steve Westbrook

Lenses on Composition Studies offers authors the unique opportunity to write for advanced undergraduate and beginning graduate students who are new to the discipline of Composition Studies. While the series aims to maintain the rigor and depth of contemporary composition scholarship, it seeks to offer this particular group of students an introduction to key disciplinary issues in accessible prose that does not assume prior advanced knowledge of scholars and theoretical debates. The series provides instructors of advanced undergraduate or beginning graduate students texts that are both appropriate and inviting for this fresh but professionally directed audience.

OTHER BOOKS IN THE SERIES
Critical Conversations About Plagiarism, edited by Michael Donnelly, Rebecca Ingalls, Tracy Ann Morse, Joanna Castner Post, and Anne Meade Stockdell-Giesler (2013)
Bibliographic Research in Composition Studies, by Vicki Byard (2009)

Composition Studies Through a Feminist Lens

Shari J. Stenberg

Parlor Press
Anderson, South Carolina
www.parlorpress.com

Parlor Press LLC, Anderson, South Carolina, USA

© 2013 by Parlor Press
All rights reserved.
Printed in the United States of America

SAN: 254-8879

Cataloging-in-Publication Data

Stenberg, Shari J.
  Composition studies through a feminist lens / Shari J. Stenberg.
    pages cm. -- (Lenses on Composition Studies)
  Includes bibliographical references and index.
    ISBN 978-1-60235-414-2 (pbk. : acid-free paper) -- ISBN 978-1-60235-415-9 (hardcover : acid-free paper) -- ISBN 978-1-60235-416-6 (adobe ebook) -- ISBN 978-1-60235-417-3 (epub)
  1. English language--Rhetoric--Study and teaching. 2. Feminism and education. I. Title.
  PE1404.S79 2013
  808'.04207--dc23
                              2013006775

1 2 3 4 5

ISBN Information
978-1-60235-414-2 (paperback)
978-1-60235-415-9 (hardcover)
978-1-60235-416-6 (Adobe eBook)
978-1-60235-417-3 (ePub)

Cover design by David Blakesley.
Printed on acid-free paper.

Parlor Press, LLC is an independent publisher of scholarly and trade titles in print and multimedia formats. This book is available in paper, cloth and eBook formats from Parlor Press on the World Wide Web at http://www.parlorpress.com or through online and brick-and-mortar bookstores. For submission information or to find out about Parlor Press publications, write to Parlor Press, 3015 Brackenberry Drive, Anderson, South Carolina, 29621, or email editor@parlorpress.com.

To the feminists who came before me, and to my daughters,
Zoe and Anika, of the next generation.

Contents

Acknowledgments *ix*

1 Composition's Origin Stories Through a Feminist Lens   *3*
   The Origin Stories of Composition Studies
     Through a Feminist Lens   *4*
   The Harvard Story: The Birth of Composition
     Studies from a Test and a Course   *6*
   For Writing and Discussion   *8*
   Classical Rhetoric as Composition's Proper Ancestor   *9*
   For Writing and Discussion   *12*
   The Process Paradigm: Composition as a Science   *12*
   For Writing and Discussion   *14*
   Looking Ahead   *14*
   Works Cited   *17*
   For Further Reading   *18*

2 The Rhetorical Tradition Through a Feminist
  Lens: Locating Women   *19*
   Locating Women among Ancient Voices: Aspasia and Diotima   *22*
   For Writing and Discussion   *24*
   Locating Available Means to Authority: Women's
     Rhetorical Challenges to the Church   *25*
   For Writing and Discussion   *27*
   Locating Women's Rhetorical Challenges to Femininity   *28*
   For Writing and Discussion   *30*
   Locating a Public Voice: The Rhetoric of the
     Suffragists and Abolitionists   *31*
   For Writing and Discussion   *34*
   Works Cited   *35*
   For Further Reading   *36*

3 Difference, Form, and Topoi Through a Feminist Lens   *38*
   Acknowledging Difference among Women   *40*
   For Writing and Discussion   *43*
   Rejecting the Master's Tools   *43*
   For Writing and Discussion   *47*
   Revising Rhetorical Contexts   *48*
   Works Cited   *49*
   For Further Reading   *50*

4 Teacher and Student Identity Through a Feminist Lens   52
   The Teacher as the (Feminized) Disciplinarian: Cleaning
      Student Texts, Cleaning Students   53
   For Writing and Discussion   55
   The Composition Teacher as (Maternal) Nurturer   56
   For Writing and Discussion   59
   Writing Teacher, Critical Teacher   59
   For Writing and Discussion   63
   Where We Are, Where We're Headed: The
      Composition Teacher as Rhetor   64
   For Writing and Discussion   66
   Works Cited   67
   For Further Reading   68

5 Research and Writing Through a Feminist
  Lens: A Focus on Experience   70
   Raising Consciousness of and about Women Writers   71
   For Writing and Discussion   74
   From Research on Gender to Feminist Research   75
   For Writing and Discussion   77
   The Evolving use of Experience   78
   For Writing and Discussion   82
   Works Cited   82
   For Further Reading   83

6 Argument Through a Feminist Lens   84
   Persuasion, Conflict, and Negotiation
      Through a Feminist Lens   85
   For Writing and Discussion   89
   Beyond the Monologic Voice   89
   For Writing and Discussion   93
   Rhetorical Listening   94
   For Writing and Discussion   97
   From Monologic to Dialogic: A Feminist
      Revision of Argument   97
   Works Cited   98
   For Further Reading   99

Epilogue   101
   Works Cited   102

Notes   103
Index   105
About the Author   109

Acknowledgments

The feminist scholars and teachers represented in this book, as well as those I work with daily, have taught me much about the possibilities of collaboration. Indeed, this book is a product of collaboration, and I'm grateful for the conversation and inspiration from others that have fueled it.

Perhaps above all, my process of developing this project has deepened my gratitude for the women in and outside of academia whose early feminist contributions now benefit all of us. Joy Ritchie is one of these women, and I'm especially thankful for her mentorship—as a scholar, colleague, and department chair. Her guidance and suggestions were a gift to me as I wrote and revised this book. I'm also grateful to Barbara DiBernard, a feminist teacher and scholar, whom I was lucky to call a colleague, and who remains a strong inspiration for my own feminist teaching and writing. Debbie Minter offers me a daily example of what it means to enact feminist leadership in the university, and her colleagueship and friendship deeply enrich my work and life.

I greatly appreciate those who read chapters of this book and offered important questions and ideas: Chris Gallagher, Jennifer Dean, and my Rhetoric of Women Writers students.

My husband, Jason, and daughters, Zoe and Anika, provide me daily doses of love and laughter that balance and feed my work. I thank them.

Finally, I want to express heartfelt appreciation to series editors Stephen Westbrook and Sheryl Fontaine for seeing the value in the project and providing thoughtful, encouraging feedback that enabled me to develop and strengthen it. I thank David Blakesley for his expert guidance of the production process and Terra Williams for her careful copyediting. They've helped make it possible for me to share with a new generation the important contributions feminists have made to Composition Studies.

Composition Studies Through a Feminist Lens

1 Composition's Origin Stories Through a Feminist Lens

We use stories to define ourselves, to create traditions, and to establish our heritage. Because Composition Studies is a relatively new discipline in the university, it has been important for its scholars to record its story, to show how it emerged and evolved and why its presence matters. As with any story, there is not just one version—and which plotlines, characters, and tensions most vividly occupy the narrative landscape depends on the lens of the storyteller. This book introduces you to stories of Composition's history, struggles, and accomplishments through the lens of feminism.

Composition Studies and feminism hold much in common. As Susan Jarratt writes:

> Both [. . .] seek to transform styles of thinking, teaching, and learning rather than to reproduce stultifying traditions. They share a suspicion of authoritarian pedagogy, emphasizing instead collaborative or interactive learning and teaching. They resist purity of approach and the reduction of their scope by moving in and around many contemporary critical theories and disciplines. (2–3)

Within both Composition and feminist scholarship, then, you are likely to find projects that value revision of classrooms, institutional politics, and knowledge practices. These projects may well be collaborative, whether involving scholars who work together to discover new knowledge or fusing knowledge from different disciplines. You are also likely to hear voices not always valued in intellectual traditions—students, community members, teachers—as well as discourse that might "sound" different from other academic writing, drawing from narrative and experience as a resource for knowledge. In fact, much of what makes Composition Studies a unique field can be traced to the infusion of feminist thought into its conversations.

By focusing a feminist lens on Composition Studies, then, this book aims to spotlight how feminist contributions have made Composition Studies a more inclusive, innovative, and exciting field. Whether illuminating difference within our classrooms and institutions or recovering and "gathering" women's voices in the rhetorical tradition, feminist contributions have created space for subjectivities previously unheard or marginalized. Feminists have introduced new methods of making arguments and engaging in research, prompting us to reevaluate what "counts" as both legitimate knowledge and legitimate subject matter for our writing. Feminist perspectives have also played a key role in broadening the field's notions of academic discourse, pointing out that restricting ourselves to traditional, Western notions of logical, linear, and objective writing consequently limits possibilities for intellectual and creative work. Finally, feminist scholars have altered our view of classrooms, underscoring the ways gender and power dynamics shape our interactions with students and offering new visions and practices for the teaching of writing.

As is probably clear by now, both feminism and Composition Studies work from values that challenge academic business as usual; consequently, both have also struggled to claim legitimacy. While the large part of this book focuses on the contributions of feminist thought to Composition Studies, this chapter examines the field's beginnings—the different ways compositionists claim the origins of the field—which illuminate ongoing tensions between maintaining countercultural values and achieving disciplinary credibility.

Now, let's return to the beginning(s).

THE ORIGIN STORIES OF COMPOSITION STUDIES THROUGH A FEMINIST LENS

When you think about Composition Studies, what comes to mind? The first English course you took at college? Practices like peer response and revision? Learning new rules and expectations for college-level writing? Or maybe, like so many English majors, you know it as the class you passed out of with an AP exam.

Although Composition Studies is now well established as a discipline with its own conferences, journals, and graduate programs, it is still most often conflated with the course from where it began: freshman writing. In fact, some scholars argue that the exact origins of the field lie in the Harvard exam of 1873, a test designed to sort out those students who needed additional training in grammar and spelling before moving on to their real coursework. Many of us who work in the field today still confront the prevailing expectation that composition teachers will—for once and for all—prepare students as writers before they enter their biology, political science, or literature classrooms. In the eyes of many, composition remains a service provider to the university. Or, looking at the field through a feminist lens, the field can be characterized as *feminized*.

I use the term *feminized* here to suggest that the work of composition, like housework or mothering, is often positioned as service work. Donna Haraway offers further explanation: to be feminized is to be "exploited as a reserve labor force" or "seen less as workers than servers" (86). This status has to do both with the work of composition teaching, which tends to be associated more with lower-status *teaching* than with higher-status *research*, as well as with the fact that teaching composition is literally women's work, since women constitute the majority of its instructors. Composition programs also tend to be staffed predominantly with part-time instructors or teaching assistants (TAs), who are commonly underpaid and overworked.

The reason this "service" status rubs many compositionists the wrong way, however, is not only because of the low standing that accompanies it but also because it conceals the different set of values that Composition Studies brings to the university, values that might be deemed as countercultural or, as I will argue, *feminist*. Sharon Crowley describes these values nicely:

> Academics who profess composition studies go about their professional work somewhat differently than do their colleagues in literary studies. Their interest in pedagogy inverts the traditional academic privileging of theory over practice and research over teaching. Composition scholarship typically focuses on the processes of learning rather than on the acquisition of knowledge, and composition pedagogy focuses on change and development in students rather than on transmission of a heritage. [. . .] Composition studies also acknowledged women's contributions to teach-

ing and scholarship long before other disciplines began to do so. (3)

As you can begin to see, then, there is a tension between composition as a *feminized* field—one that tends to be defined and sometimes controlled by others—and as a *feminist* field—one that values teaching and learning, difference, collaboration, and process.

In order to give you a clearer view of this tension, I'll now describe three of the field's origin stories. I have chosen origin stories because, as with families or even individuals, narratives of how we came to be play an important role in self-definition and identity; this is certainly the case with the field of Composition Studies. These stories will serve as narrative touchstones to which I will return as I show, throughout the book, how feminists have challenged and revised them. I'll begin with the story of the previously mentioned Harvard exam, which left a legacy the field would perpetually try to undo by telling new stories about itself. The problem, as you'll see, is that sometimes the way these stories are constructed—so as to lend the field more credibility—tends to discredit the field's feminist contributions and/or values. So in this chapter I'll also point to some of the ways feminist scholars have responded to these origin stories, inserting or reclaiming alternative values, often by drawing from feminist ideas across disciplines or even outside the academy.

THE HARVARD STORY: THE BIRTH OF COMPOSITION STUDIES FROM A TEST AND A COURSE

As you likely know from experience, tests are designed not only to measure learning but also to track and separate students into categories, to reward prior learning and backgrounds, and sometimes to determine how well teachers are instructing students. In the case of the 1873 Harvard exam, the test aimed to accomplish all of these functions. The need for the exam in the first place came about when Harvard president Charles William Eliot opened admission to "students in all conditions of life," that is, to high school graduates educated in free (public) high schools, as opposed to only those graduates of elite preparatory schools (qtd. in Douglas 128). At the same time he wanted to welcome a wider range of students, Eliot also sought to ensure that those students who received a Harvard education were of "promising ability and best character" (128).

Chapter 1: Composition's Origin Stories Through a Feminist Lens

Since social class was tied to character, the written entrance exam served to sort the refined—the traditional Harvard applicant—from the unrefined—the new (lower class) demographic seeking college education. A student's grammatical usage, then, became indicative of his social identity. Those students whose usage departed from valued standards were considered dirty, unrefined, and unmannered—and sent to freshman composition, which functioned as an inoculation of correct grammar and spelling (Miller 52). Within these courses, students no longer wrote argument or exposition, but instead composed pieces considered less abstract and complex that could, as Robert J. Connors puts it, "be quickly scanned for obvious flaws" (*Composition-Rhetoric* 141). Teachers marked these papers using symbols that corresponded to a "correction card," a reference students used to remedy each grammatical offense (144). Ultimately, the point of the required course was not, Crowley contends, "to acquire some level of skill or knowledge" to be measured upon exit, but it was instead "to subject students to discipline, to force them to recognize the power of the institution and to insist on conformity with its standards" (74).

What Eliot and his colleagues didn't expect was that over half of the Harvard students (*including* many of those from elite preparatory schools) would fail the exam. Not only did this heighten the need for a first-year composition class, it also placed heavy pressure on the high school teachers to improve their students' performance (or, we might say, improve the students, themselves). The situation escalated to a full-blown literacy crisis when Harvard published the condemning results of its exam in *The Dial*, a popular national journal. The eventual result was an 1894 National Conference on Uniform Entrance Requirements, which established a list of texts for use in college English entrance exams that effectively determined the secondary school curriculum—and therefore, the teachers' work (Graff 99).

While it was male university administrators feminizing (at that time largely male) instructors of college composition, those who ultimately bore the brunt of the "literacy crisis" were the mostly female secondary school teachers, who were blamed for failing to adequately prepare students for college. That is, the literal feminization of American schooling—women constituted sixty-three percent of America's teachers by 1888, and ninety percent in cities (Grumet 34)—coincided with a presumed literacy crisis at the university level, and ultimately with the feminization of composition. As early as 1929, in fact, a survey of teaching conditions in freshman English indicates that women conducted thirty-eight percent of composition instruction nationwide, constituting the highest percentage of female instruction in any college discipline, with the exception of home economics (Connors, "Overwork" 121).

The Harvard origin story—with students deemed unable to meet (often unnamed) requirements and teachers bearing the blame—echoes throughout composition's history. The implications are many. Just as the late nineteenth-century college administrators told high school English teachers what to teach, first-year composition and high school teachers alike often lack control over their own curricula. Further, because US educational history is laden with perceived "literacy crises"—the ongoing notion that "these students can't write"—first-year writing has been, and continues to be, in high demand. To meet this demand, universities typically staff first-year writing courses with TAs and adjunct instructors (the greatest percentage of whom are women), who are underpaid and overworked.

To make visible and respond to these issues, feminists in Composition Studies have conducted studies and launched important arguments about the literal feminization of composition, raising awareness about labor and work conditions for part-time instructors (Enos; Holbrook; Miller; Schell). In so doing, they call attention to institutional dynamics that position the (especially part-time) composition teacher as the "proverbial housewife who contributes greatly to the running of the household (or the university) but gets no actual recognition for it (e.g. tenure, salary increases, office space, resources)" (Schell 554–55). Feminists in composition have also sought to challenge the metaphorical feminization of teaching in the university, arguing that teaching is intellectual work deserving of status equal to research.

Because of its historical connection to first-year writing, composition—to this day—is often associated first and foremost with the feminized work of teaching. As you'll see in the stories that follow, the field has sought to claim alternative origins that establish its identity within the more masculine terms of the research university.

For Writing and Discussion

1. Have you ever taken a high-stakes writing test (say, determining entrance into a program or course or determining your

placement in a curriculum)? What knowledge or skills did it ask you to demonstrate? Based on this, what assumptions can you make about the nature of the knowledge or practices the test valued? What can and cannot be measured by such an exam? Which test takers might be most advantaged or disadvantaged by these tests?

2. First-year writing is a course about which many groups feel compelled to voice their opinion. Do a media search for news about student writing or a "literacy crisis." What do you find? How are problems with student writing framed? What does this framing tell you about what is most valued when it comes to writing? How might these values be read as gendered?

3. Take a look at several first-year writing program websites around the country. Look at who teaches the courses and how they are categorized (faculty, instructors, TAs). What can you tell about the labor conditions at work? Who does most of the teaching? What is the gender division among teachers or between tenure track and part-time instructors?

CLASSICAL RHETORIC AS COMPOSITION'S PROPER ANCESTOR

During the mid twentieth century, the organization of US universities assumed a formation we're familiar with today—one divided by disciplines and within those disciplines, sorted by professors' specialties. With professors occupied by their own research, the bulk of first-year composition teaching fell to TAs and part-time instructors; or, as Richard M. Weaver described the situation in 1963, composition courses were staffed by "just about anyone" who would teach it, including "beginners, part-time teachers, graduate students, faculty wives, and various fringe people" (qtd. in Crowley 119).

With the business of teaching assigned to women and associated with caretaking and drudgery, those interested in professionalizing the field needed to legitimize it by locating something other than teaching at its center. One strategy was to tell a new story about the field's origins, replacing composition's ancestry as a fix-it shop for poor student writing with the noble paternal lineage of classical rhetoric. From this thinking emerged what James Berlin dubs "The Renaissance of

Rhetoric" or what Susan Miller, through a more critical lens, calls composition's "neoclassical account" of its history. According to this story, then, the origins of composition exist not in the feminized act of teaching a service course, but in venerated figures like Plato and Aristotle and canonical works of classical rhetoric.

Restoring rhetoric to university education would not only give composition a legitimate history, subject matter, and research area but some scholars believed it would also help revise the focus and purpose of composition instruction, altering the curricular focus from correctness to Aristotelian argument. This movement marks a moment when scholars like Albert R. Kitzhaber, Wayne C. Booth, and Ken Macrorie, from within the field itself, aimed to define the field's pedagogical and scholarly contours. It connected the teaching of composition to a rich, established tradition that involved careful study and deployment of rhetorical concepts: ethos, logos, audience, purpose, style. Edward P. J. Corbett's *Classical Rhetoric for the Modern Student* is the best known of this scholarship. Here Corbett sought to reclaim the fifth-century approaches for the contemporary classroom. This system "taught the student how to find something to say, how to select and organize his material, and how to phrase it in the best possible way" (vii). Indeed, this process may resonate with some writing pedagogies you've experienced, where you locate a topic, gather research, create an outline to arrange it, and then write the paper.

In Corbett's textbook, students first focus on "Discovery of Arguments" by practicing thesis formation and ways to "appeal to reason." They also learn that sometimes it is necessary to appeal to emotion, since Corbett acknowledges that while "rationality is man's essential characteristic," man is also moved by "irrational motives" (39). Once students have determined what they want to say, they are led through the process of arrangement: introduction, statement of fact, confirmation, and conclusion. Finally, Corbett addresses issues of style, which range from "grammatical competence," to "choice of diction," to sentence structure and word order. At the root of this approach is the belief that rhetoric should occupy the center of composition classrooms because of its omnipresence in our society; students must make and respond to arguments in their daily lives. Corbett also suggests that a rhetorical approach highlights persuasive devices that "come naturally, instinctively to human beings" (30), which could be honed by opportunities to study and practice this activity.

Others, though, highlighted limitations to this tactic. As Miller, as well as C. H. Knoblauch and Lil Brannon, points out, many of these efforts to establish classical rhetoric as a predecessor to modern composition failed to complicate the seemingly generic or universal "rational" subject at its center, who was, in fact, a male subject from the ruling elite. Women in ancient Greece were denied education, literacy, and citizenship, and in fact, weren't even allowed into the public sphere, let alone to make public arguments. Likewise, this discourse presents "rationalism," which is foundational to effective persuasion, as a natural human attribute. For instance, in Corbett's words, "Rationality is man's essential characteristic" (39). Consequently, alternative ways of knowing or being in the world are easily deemed irrational, alien, or illegitimate.

Feminist scholars have also challenged the idea that practices of classical oratory can simply transfer across centuries, geography, and populations. We see this assumption in Corbett's treatment of a scene from *The Iliad* in his textbook. From this text, he argues, the "modern student" learns that "despite the hundreds of years that separate his society from Homer's, men acted and responded then in much the same way that they do today" (19). Even as the "dominant ideas of society change," Corbett argues that "the basic human passions and motivations are the same today as they were in Homer's day" (19). As you'll see in the chapters ahead, feminist scholars place great emphasis—whether recovering ancient rhetorical texts or addressing contemporary classrooms—on the importance of local contexts and attention to differences within them, thereby disrupting the idea of universal rhetorical strategies or human characteristics.

While ancient rhetorical practices were never widely adopted in the composition classroom, the study of rhetoric would continue to be a vital line of inquiry in the field—one that has often been privileged above composition as a "practical," feminine classroom subject. For instance, in a survey Theresa Enos conducted in the 1980s on gender and publishing in Composition and Rhetoric, she found a split within "rhetoric" and "composition," such that scholarship in rhetoric was associated with knowledge production (i.e., the territory of men), while scholarship in composition connoted a focus on pedagogy, and was therefore more open to women.

Beginning in the 1990s, however, feminist scholars began to challenge the notion of a "unified" rhetoric attributed solely to classical male figures and designated as the scholarly territory of male scholars. Feminist conceptions of rhetoric, or "rhetorica," as Andrea A. Lunsford has dubbed this work, interrupt the "seamless narratives" of the rhetorical tradition, refusing to valorize "one, traditional, competitive, agonistic, and linear mode of rhetorical discourse" (6). Instead, Lunsford writes, feminist rhetoric makes room for multiplicity—for rhetorics—and for "dangerous moves" (often equated with the feminine) such as "breaking the silence, naming in personal terms, employing dialogics, recognizing and using the power of conversation, moving centripetally toward connections and valuing—indeed insisting upon—collaboration" (6). In this way, then, feminist rhetorics extended the texts that comprised (and were taught as) the "rhetorical tradition," altered accepted rhetorical strategies, and expanded possibilities for writing instruction and practice.

For Writing and Discussion

1. Has education in rhetoric been part of your own learning experience? If so, how would you describe the way rhetoric was represented?
2. Doing a search on the Internet, take a look at several composition programs that espouse a rhetorical focus for their curriculum. In what ways does the program reclaim classical rhetoric? In what ways does it disrupt it or move beyond it?

The Process Paradigm: Composition as a Science

Because the humanities are often deemed "soft" (or feminine) in relation to the "hard" sciences, one way English studies has sought to legitimize itself as a discipline is to claim connections to science. Within literary studies, we can see an example of this during the 1940s and 1950s when New Criticism flourished. New Criticism involved examining the text as an isolated artifact—rather than connecting it to the author's biography or historical moment, as was the established practice at the time—and then analyzing it using a technical, field-specific vocabulary.

In order to rewrite its central identity as a discipline, and not merely a service course, composition scholars also sought scientific affiliation

Chapter 1: Composition's Origin Stories Through a Feminist Lens

by locating a subject that could be scientifically studied: the writing process. For some narrators of composition's history, then, the field's origins as a discipline began with its research focus.

One example of composition's efforts to achieve scientific status came in 1961 when NCTE (National Council of Teachers of English) created an ad hoc committee to prepare a "scientifically based report" on the status of knowledge in the teaching and learning of composition. In so doing, the committee developed criteria for what counted as research that made "genuine contributions to knowledge": research that studied the process of written instruction using scientific methods with the goal of improving composition teaching (North, "Death" 198). The resulting document, *Research in Written Composition*, by Richard Braddock, Richard Lloyd-Jones, and Lowell Schoer, served as what Stephen M. North calls the "charter of modern Composition" (*Making* 17). The book insists that teaching-based inquiry needs to be replaced with scientific methodology. As the text states:

> the field as a whole is laced with dreams, prejudices and makeshift operations. Not enough investigators are really informing themselves about the process and results of previous research before embarking on their own. Too few of them conduct pilot experiments and validate their measuring instruments before undertaking an investigation. [. . .] And far too few of those who have conducted an initial piece of research follow it with further exploration or replicate the investigations of others. (5)

Teachers, then, were replaced by "investigators" as the central agents of the field. Knowledge derived from classroom experience was replaced with the stuff of science—pilot experiments, measuring instruments, and replicated studies.

While this emphasis on scientific approaches did allow Composition Studies to advance its status as a discipline and gain legitimacy in and outside of English studies, it also deepened the fracture between largely male researchers who studied composition and female teachers who practiced it in the classroom with students. Consequently, a top-down dynamic was created where male researchers produced scholarship that directed female teachers about how best to teach. In the decades that followed, the number of women hired in tenure-track (research) positions in composition would continue to grow, but a divide remains between those who teach the bulk of composition courses and those who conduct research—a split that feminist scholars, among others, continue to critique and challenge.

Finally, the emphasis on science limited the definition of what counts as legitimate "knowledge," a question that is central to the feminist project. While composition scholarship certainly diversified over time in both its subjects of study—moving far beyond how to teach first-year composition—and in the form its research assumes, the privileging of seemingly "objective" and quantitative research in the university looms large, even today. One such consequence of this hierarchy is that scholarship focused on teaching is often deemed "soft" or less rigorous than other forms of research. For this reason, it remains an ongoing part of the feminist project to challenge what kind of and whose knowledge we privilege in order to make room for new voices, perspectives, and subjects.

For Writing and Discussion

1. What evidence do you see in the academy that demonstrates the privileging of scientific knowledge? What evidence do you see where other forms of knowledge have successfully challenged the limitations of science?

2. In what ways might scientific approaches to work in fields like English studies serve us? In what ways does it limit us?

Looking Ahead

As this glimpse into the competing origin stories of Composition Studies shows, the field has long sought to revise the status that links it to remediation and feminization. In establishing disciplinary and pedagogical agency, however, the field has sometimes claimed origins that exclude or marginalize feminist knowledges. For this reason, feminist teachers and scholars have had to regularly disrupt, challenge, and offer alternatives to the field's efforts to establish disciplinarity. In the chapters ahead, I provide an overview of feminist contributions to Composition and Rhetoric, which both revise these origin stories and offer a more expansive and inclusive view of how we understand writers and rhetors, writing and rhetoric, and teaching and learning in the field.

In the first section of the book, Chapters 2 and 3, I highlight feminist scholars' efforts to alter the rhetorical tradition, described in the second origin story above. While feminist revisions of the rhetorical tradition emerged later, chronologically, than feminist contributions to the composition classroom, I begin with a look at "rhetorica" because, as you'll see, the recovered rhetorics of women from across centuries show approaches, knowledges, and values upon which feminists in Rhetoric and Composition would continue to build—implicitly and explicitly—in both their writing and in their classrooms.

Chapters 2 and 3 show how feminists have called attention to the masculinist, class-stratified cultures in which ancient rhetorics emerged, which helps us approach these texts with greater awareness of whom, and what, they exclude. Feminists have also argued that rhetoric need not be limited to these classical, canonized texts. Instead, they have reclaimed and rewritten the tradition by recovering women's voices that have been previously overlooked or forgotten. They invite us to ask, what does it mean to locate our origins within the context of a more inclusive, diversified, feminist rhetoric? Chapter 2 features a range of voices feminists have recovered, which changes the sound, purpose, and tradition of rhetoric. Chapter 3 focuses on more contemporary feminist rhetorical projects that move away from a focus on individual voices to celebrate and investigate common themes and tropes across women's rhetorics, including attention to human diversity, multiplicity of forms, and new rhetorical topoi, or the topics and places from which arguments can be made. Together, these feminist rhetorical contributions open new possibilities for how we teach, learn, and participate in the rhetorical tradition.

In Part 2 of the book, I focus on how feminist compositionists have expanded traditional notions of teacher and student roles, the practices and persona of the researcher, and approaches to academic argument. In each case, feminist compositionists emphasize the importance of how social location and subjectivity—how subjects are situated according to gender, power, race, embodiment, etc.—shape how we know, teach, learn, and write. That is, just as feminist rhetors challenge the idea of universal rhetorical practices or effects, feminist compositionists emphasize that how we experience our world, our communities, our classrooms, depends on our particular location within it; and that location is necessarily shaped by gender, which is always enmeshed with other social categories.

In Chapter 4 I illustrate how feminists in composition have influenced the field's perception of the teacher and the student. In this chapter, I trace key metaphors for the composition teacher, and subsequent roles for students, which emerge from several pedagogical movements. I then highlight how feminist scholars have complicated these identities, illuminating the gendered assumptions that shape them and making room for more inclusive, expansive notions of teacher and student identities. In so doing, feminists in composition revise the role of service-provider or disciplinarian established in the first origin story.

Chapter 5 depicts a feminist response to the third origin story, which aimed to legitimize the field by associating it with objective, scientific knowledge. Here I trace feminist efforts to challenge the idealized persona in academic writing and settings, which is built upon a scientific model of the objective, logical, rational—that is, masculine—knower. Alternatively, feminist scholars have sought to claim the subjectivity of the writer and researcher, arguing for experience as a vital form of knowledge.

Chapter 6 highlights how feminists in composition have revised conventional expectations about what constitutes academic writing. Even as Composition Studies grew as a field and gained more agency in defining its courses and curriculum, an ongoing pressure remains to prepare students for all of their other courses. In this chapter, I'll explore how feminists have challenged notions of argument and the unified, monologic voice it privileges, instead advocating for collaboration, inquiry, and for the importance of listening as much as persuading.

While feminist scholarship in Composition and Rhetoric has tended to move in two parallel, though sometimes intersecting, directions—one with a focus on feminist rhetorical texts and practices and one with a focus on writing, pedagogy, and curricula within universities—I highlight throughout the chapters ahead how the two function reciprocally to enhance research, teaching, and writing in Composition and Rhetoric. Indeed, through these contributions, rhetorical and pedagogical, feminists in the field have rewritten the story of composition.

Works Cited

Berlin, James. *Rhetoric and Reality: Writing Instruction in American Colleges, 1900–1985*. Carbondale: Southern Illinois UP, 1987. Print.

Braddock, Richard, Richard Lloyd-Jones, and Lowell Schoer. *Research in Written Composition*. Champaign, IL: NCTE, 1963. Print.

Connors, Robert J. *Composition-Rhetoric: Backgrounds, Theory, and Pedagogy*. Pittsburgh, PA: U of Pittsburgh P, 1997. Print.

—. "Overwork/Underpay: Labor and Status of Composition Teachers Since 1880." *Rhetoric Review* 9.1 (1990): 108–26. Print.

Corbett, Edward P. J. *Classical Rhetoric for the Modern Student*. New York: Oxford UP, 1971. Print.

Crowley, Sharon. *Composition in the University: Historical and Polemical Essays*. Pittsburgh, PA: U of Pittsburgh P, 1998. Print.

Douglas, Wallace. "Rhetoric for the Meritocracy." *English in America*. Ed. Richard Ohmann. New York: Oxford UP, 1976. 97–132. Print.

Enos, Theresa. "Gender and Publishing Scholarship in Rhetoric and Composition." *Feminism and Composition: A Critical Sourcebook*. Ed. Gesa Kirsch et al. Boston, MA: Bedford/St. Martin's, 2003. 558–72. Print.

Graff, Gerald. *Professing Literature: An Institutional History*. Chicago, IL: U of Chicago P, 1987. Print.

Grumet, Madeleine R. *Bitter Milk: Women and Teaching*. Amherst: U of Massachusetts P, 1988. Print.

Haraway, Donna. "A Manifesto for Cyborgs: Science, Technology, and Social Feminism in the 1980s." *Socialist Review* 14.2 (1985): 65–107. Print.

Holbrook, Sue Ellen. "Women's Work: The Feminization of Composition Studies." *Rhetoric Review* 9 (1991): 201–29. Print.

Jarratt, Susan C. "Introduction." *Feminism and Composition Studies: In Other Words*. Ed. Susan C. Jarratt and Lynn Worsham. New York: MLA, 1998. 1–18. Print.

Knoblauch, C.H., and Lil Brannon. *Rhetorical Traditions and the Teaching of Writing*. Portsmouth, NH: Boynton/Cook, 1984. Print.

Lunsford, Andrea A. *Reclaiming Rhetorica: Women in the Rhetorical Tradition*. Pittsburgh, PA: U of Pittsburgh P, 1995. Print.

Miller, Susan. *Textual Carnivals: The Politics of Composition*. Carbondale: Southern Illinois UP, 1991. Print.

North, Stephen M. "The Death of Paradigm Hope, the End of Paradigm Guilt, and the Future of (Research in) Composition." *Composition in the Twenty-First Century: Crisis and Change*. Ed. Lynn Z. Bloom, Donald A. Daiker, and Edward White. Carbondale: Southern Illinois UP, 1996. 194–207. Print.

—. *The Making of Knowledge in Composition: Portrait of an Emerging Field*. Portsmouth, NH: Boynton/Cook, 1987. Print.

Schell, Eileen. *Gypsy Academics and Mother-Teachers: Gender, Contingent Labor, and Writing Instruction*. Portsmouth, NH: Boynton/Cook, 1997. Print.

For Further Reading

Berlin, James. *Rhetoric and Reality: Writing Instruction in American Colleges, 1900–1985*. Carbondale: Southern Illinois UP, 1987. Print.

Crowely, Sharon. *Composition in the University: Historical and Polemical Essays*. Pittsburgh, PA: U of Pittsburgh P, 1998. Print.

Holbrook, Sue Ellen. "Women's Work: The Feminization of Composition Studies." *Rhetoric Review* 9 (1991): 201–29. Print.

Miller, Susan. "The Feminization of Composition." *Feminism and Composition: A Critical Sourcebook*. Ed. Gesa Kirsch et al. Boston, MA: Bedford/St. Martin's, 2003. 520–33. Print.

2 The Rhetorical Tradition Through a Feminist Lens: Locating Women

Rhetoric has a complex reputation. To some, it is a venerated, classical tradition—a two-thousand-year-old centerpiece of western education, and the cornerstone of effective public discourse and persuasion. To others, the term rhetoric signifies empty political discourse, or worse, a tool of nasty, partisan politics. A quick Google news search on "rhetoric," for instance, yields phrases like this: "GOP full of empty rhetoric"; "his campaign is full of rhetoric that doesn't amount to much"; "US officials deploy increasingly aggressive rhetoric"; "Obama's rhetorical onslaught"; and "politicians stepped up 'tough on crime' rhetoric." This tells us that, at least within mainstream media, rhetoric denotes speech that is public and political, uttered by powerful figures, sometimes devoid of meaning, and often agonistic or argumentative. Still others approach rhetoric as vehicle for argument and agency—a way to make one's voice heard, to sponsor change. This, in fact, is how contemporary scholars in Composition and Rhetoric tend to view rhetorical engagement. Here, rhetoric is writing and speaking that creates and communicates knowledge; rhetorical strategies (i.e., how a text is organized, what evidence is used, what kind of voice is employed) are necessarily shaped by cultural assumptions about language, knowledge, and reality. By examining what kinds of rhetorical practices are most predominant at a given time, we learn much about the values, assumptions, and social and political contexts of its users. As James Berlin notes, however, rhetoric is not a unitary field. "While one particular rhetorical theory may predominate at any historical moment, none remains dominant over time; thus, we ought not to talk about *rhetoric* but [. . .] of *rhetorics*" (3).

Indeed, women writers and feminist scholars have played an important role in revising the idea of a unitary masculine rhetoric, since, as Cheryl Glenn notes, the tradition of classical rhetoric is often problematically conceived of "great men speaking out" (52). Historically, rhetorical acts were categorized as *"exclusively* upper-class, male, agonistic, and public—yet seemingly universal" (2). While "universal" implies that any speaker could enter the rhetorical sphere, the definition of rhetoric as public, competitive acts of persuasion long excluded women from rhetorical participation. Women have historically been denied public speech, education, and literacy—and in fact, in some cultures, are still denied—making it difficult, and sometimes nearly impossible, to speak and to be heard.

Despite these conditions, feminist scholars have successfully demonstrated that we can hear women's voices in the tradition(s) if we listen hard enough, or, in some cases, if we listen for different *kinds* of rhetoric. Thanks to the work of these scholars, an extensive revision of the rhetorical tradition is underway, as they recover women's voices, and in so doing, alter the very definition of rhetoric.

In this chapter, I provide a sampling of the voices feminist rhetors have recovered, beginning with the texts that have now become what Joy Ritchie and Kate Ronald call "the primary works" of feminist rhetoric. These voices include overlooked female figures from ancient rhetoric, like Aspasia and Diotima, and early female theologians, like Julian of Norwich and Margery Kempe. These voices also stem from the suffragist and abolitionist movements. While we may have learned about figures like Susan B. Anthony or Sojourner Truth in our history books, feminist rhetoricians help us consider how these women were rhetoricians in their own right, borrowing and appropriating rhetorical strategies to participate in the public sphere.

As I showed in the last chapter, one of the ways Composition Studies has sought to establish itself as a discipline is by claiming its historical roots in rhetoric. The work of recovering women's voices to the rhetorical tradition, then, has much to do with writing instruction, which is central to composition. Whether or not classical rhetoric is composition's ancestor, the *values* of masculine classical rhetoric have forcefully shaped what we in contemporary western culture consider good argument and writing: linear, persuasive, objective-sounding, and clear. The classical tradition also shapes the assumed purpose of rhetoric: to win. As Robert J. Connors observes, "Classical rhetoric is, plain and simple, about fighting [. . .] Rhetoric was about contest and struggle; indeed, *agonistikos* as used by Aristotle in the *Rhetoric* means 'fit for athletic contests' (1.5.14) as well as 'fit for debating' (3.12.1)" (27).

A look back on the culture of the ancient rhetoricians helps illuminate the purposes and practices that gave rise to such values. For Plato and Aristotle, rhetoric was ideally a means to "win the souls" of their listeners—to ensure that Truth prevailed. Consider how Richard Weaver, a twentieth-century rhetorical scholar, summarizes Plato's view of the rhetorician: "The rhetorician will have such a high moral purpose in all his work that he will ever be chiefly concerned about saying that which is 'acceptable to God.' [. . .] The perfect rhetorician, as a philosopher, knows the will of God" (qtd. in Golden, Berquist, and Coleman 20). Subsequently, this perfect rhetorician could employ language to directly translate God's will to his audience.

With stakes as high as "winning souls," it was imperative that the rhetor avoid using "false" rhetoric—rhetoric that relied on emotional appeal or colorful language, say—and instead employ "true" rhetoric, which was deemed pure and transparent, *delivering* but not *interpreting* a message. (Here you see some origins of a cultural privileging of "objective" language, for media that is "fair and balanced" and for research papers with no "I.") To accomplish this, Plato offers a highly controlled approach to true rhetoric, which requires the speaker to 1) know the truth of his argument; 2) know what will be persuasive to a particular audience; 3) define his terms, knowing what is and is not debatable; 4) order and arrange his language, with a clear beginning and end; 5) employ proper decorum, emphasizing clarity, brevity, and simplicity (Golden, Berquist, and Coleman 20). We see this structure reflected in Edward P. J. Corbett's 1965 *Classical Rhetoric for the Modern Student*, which separates and orders the work of arguments into four parts: introduction, discovery of argument, arrangement of material, and style.

While the ancients considered the work of establishing a chain of logical propositions (philosophy) more important than the language of delivery, decorum—clarity, succinctness, appropriateness—was crucial to the ancients in much the same way "correct" writing remains a priority in many classrooms today. Because the classical rhetorician was a privileged citizen, often enlightening the non-educated, his rhetoric served as a display of privilege, status, and honor. To move outside of "correct" logic and language, then, demonstrated questionable moral status.

We can see this demonstrated in Plato's and Aristotle's low regard for the Sophists, a group of fifth-century teachers who offered (for pay) instruction in persuasion and oratory and who viewed truth not as predetermined but as constructed in each distinct context. Rather than relying on strict notions of "true" rhetoric, the Sophists utilized a wide range of discursive practices, many of which would fall into Plato's category of "false" rhetoric. In fact, As Susan C. Jarratt contends, Plato and Aristotle critiqued many characteristics of Sophistic rhetoric that are also present in feminist rhetoric: "generic diversity, loose organization, a reliance on narrative, physical pleasure in language production and reception, a holistic psychology of communication, and an emphasis on the aural relationship between speaker and listener" (72). The valorization of Plato and Aristotle—and their emphasis on a highly linear, "objective," logic-based rhetoric—remains today, and it shapes whose voices are heard, recorded, and taught.

This makes the addition of female voices to the rhetorical tradition all the more significant, because they ask us to think in new ways about what counts as legitimate knowledge, argument, and speech acts. They help us to see that what is often assumed to be "good writing" and "good speech" is indeed a result of what Patricia Bizzell calls "the cultural preferences of the most powerful people in the community" (1). In this way, then, the inclusion of women's voices is not simply additive; women's voices raise new questions, alter history, offer social critique, and they also make space for new kinds of knowledge and new kinds of writing.

Locating Women among Ancient Voices: Aspasia and Diotima

For feminist scholars, the connection of composition's historical origins to classical rhetoric raises concerns. They challenge the idea that classical rhetoric is a universal guide to good speech and writing, showing how it stemmed from exclusivity—a training ground for the male ruling class. The near absence of women in classical rhetoric transpires from the fact that women in fifth-century Athens were utterly silenced—in fact, because women were denied citizenship, the language did not even have a word for a women from Athens (Loraux 10). Women were deprived of education, literacy, citizenship, and even entry to the public sphere, except during religious festivals. In the words of Aristotle, "between the sexes, the male is by nature superior and the female inferior, the male ruler and the female subject" (1.2.12 *Politics*, qtd. in Glenn 50). Considering these conditions for women, it's remarkable that feminist scholars have recovered Aspasia and Diotima, two women who contributed to rhetoric and philosophy in Ancient Greece.

Born in Miletus (now Turkey) in fifth century BCE, Aspasia somehow achieved literacy before immigrating to Athens, where she was considered an exotic "foreigner." In Athens Aspasia served as a rhetorician, philosopher, political influence, and teacher of male rhetoricians. There are no direct records of Aspasia's voice; instead, her influence and speech is rendered through the words of men. For instance, in a dialogue between Menexenus and Socrates, Socrates claims that he has in Aspasia "an excellent mistress in the art of rhetoric—she who has made so many good speakers, and one who was the best among all the Hellenes—Pericles, the son of Xanthippus" (*Menexenus* par. 235, qtd. in Jarratt and Ong 15).

Pericles, whom Socrates deems "the best among all the Hellenes," was Aspasia's lover, a detail that has served to delegitimize her influence. After all, the ideal Greek woman was silent, with a closed mouth and closed body. Aspasia defied both of these traits, and so history has often written her as "self-indulgent, licentious, immoral" (Glenn 39). In fact, there was much about Aspasia that transgressed social norms of the time, including her unique relationship to Pericles. According to Susan Jarratt and Rory Ong, Athenian women who were not slaves were defined by their relationship to men: as wives (who brought dowries to increase family wealth); concubines (who served as sexual companions for men); or hetaerae (who accompanied men to public festivities) (12). Aspasia fit none of these roles. Instead, she served as the divorced Pericles's "beloved and constant companion" as well as his intellectual equal and teacher (12).

Perhaps Aspasia's most notable rhetorical contribution—at least to our knowledge—is her likely authorship of the famous funeral oration in Plato's *Menexenus*. In the dialogue preceding the oration, Socrates states, "Pericles spoke, but [. . .] she composed" (Aspasia 3). The speech glorifies Athens and its heroic ancestors, crediting women for their role in reproducing Greek soldiers. In this way, it is not so much Aspasia's words—as spoken through Plato—that challenge social norms of the time, it is rather Aspasia's very presence, as a woman, foreigner, and intellectual, that inadvertently disrupts the words attributed to her. It is her existence as a rhetorician, philosopher, and teacher within a male tradition that asks us to pay closer attention to the silences and absences in rhetorical history.

Like Aspasia, Diotima is another exceptional female presence in the texts of classical rhetoric. Also like Aspasia, Diotima's voice is only audible through male ancient rhetors—and now amplified through the words and imaginations of feminist scholars. We know of Diotima through the words of Socrates in Plato's *Symposium*, and consequently, historians have questioned her existence at all. As Glenn argues, however, "Whether Diotima was historical or literary [. . .] seems not as important as her having been a female influence on both Socrates and Plato" (48).

Within the *Symposium*, Diotima contributes to the speeches on love, defining love as an intermediate spirit that moves through discourse between the gods and humans. She likens love to philosophy, ultimately leading one to ideals and ideas. To reach this version of love, one begins with eros, desire for the beautiful and beautiful individuals, then ascends to beautiful ideas, and then "culminates in love for the reproduction and expression of those ideas" (qtd. in Glenn 46). For Diotima the "product" of love—or connection among subjects—is not biological reproduction, but the production of "beauty's values and ideas" (46). Love, then, is a means to discourse and dialogue, with greater intellect and ideas as the ultimate goal. As C. Jan Swearingen writes of Diotima, "She develops views and positions in a speech; she questions traditional views; and she dissents from those who have preceded her in a dialogue" (46).

Although we hear the voices of Aspasia and Diotima through male orators, the attention feminist scholars bring to their work allows us to imagine the rhetorical tradition as influenced by women's ideas and instruction.

For Writing and Discussion

1. Feminist scholars argue that the mere *presence* of women in the rhetorical tradition marks a significant shift in our understanding of classical rhetoric—even if, as other scholars contend, these women simply served as mouthpieces for male rhetors. Where do you stand on this issue? Can the same be ar-

gued today? Is female presence in a predominantly male arena enough to disrupt gendered norms, or do women also need to explicitly challenge prevailing attitudes about women to make a difference?

2. Cheryl Glenn argues that Diotima's influence on Socrates is ultimately more important than historical facts about her. Why do you think she makes this case? Do you agree? Why or why not?

LOCATING AVAILABLE MEANS TO AUTHORITY: WOMEN'S RHETORICAL CHALLENGES TO THE CHURCH

While women of the Middle Ages were excluded from engaging in public discourse and typically denied education, some found access to authority and literacy by working within and against the structures of the Christian church. Here I focus on just two of those women, Julian of Norwich and Margery Kempe, who were born thirty years apart; each offers an important example of women who used rhetorical skills in and outside of the church to make room for female experience within Christianity. In so doing, they also disrupted traditional rhetorical practice.

During the Middle Ages, the convent provided the most likely means for women to achieve literacy. Julian of Norwich (1343–1415), who was presumably a convent educated Benedictine nun, wrote a book called *Revelations of Divine Love Showed to a Devout Ankress* at a time when most people could not read or write. Like other mystics at the time, including Paul and Augustine, Julian's theological authority stemmed from dramatic visions of the Passion that came to her during a severe illness. She then expounded upon these visions, using them to establish her credibility and to create a foundation for her theological contributions. As Glenn argues, "her religious disclosures take her further than membership in the [mystic] tradition: the understanding, interpretation, and precise recording of her mystical revelations entitle her to join the ranks of Christian rhetors" (97).

There is much about her writing that makes it exceptional. In addition to its "meticulous organization and literary skill [that rank her] with Chaucer as a pioneering genius of English prose" (Janzen 15, qtd. in Glenn 94), Julian wrote in vernacular English that invites her audience *into* a conversation rather than speaks *for* it, as did most theological work at the time. In this way, Julian aimed to widen the circle of Christian participation by emphasizing the connection between God and humanity. She writes, "I saw no difference between God and our substance, but as it were, all God; and still my understanding accepted that our substance is in God, that is to say that God is God, and our substance is a creature in God" (qtd. in Glenn 97).

Perhaps most notable for the purposes of feminist rhetoric is her rewriting of God as both mother and father, and further, her configuration of Jesus as a woman, calling him "our true mother" and arguing that he is "where the ground of motherhood begins, with all the sweet protection of love which follows eternally" (Julian of Norwich 26). By reimagining the divine as feminine and demonstrating what Glenn calls "complete ease with being a female interpreter of the divine" (98), Julian makes room for women to participate and intervene in the Christian tradition.

While her work was not likely well known during her life, we do know that she influenced another female mystic, Margery Kempe, who visited Julian for advice about her own visions. Kempe went on to write—or more accurately, to narrate to a scribe, as she could not read or write—a spiritual autobiography called *The Book of Margery Kempe*. Unlike her female contemporary authors, Kempe was a layperson. She grew up in England, the daughter of a prominent family, then married a merchant and mothered fourteen children. As Glenn notes, Kempe's book "gives voice to a largely silent and unsung force, the voice of the middle-class, uneducated woman determined to be understood on her own terms: 'I preach not [. . .]; I come into no pulpit. I use but communication and good words, and that I will do while I live'" (104).

Her autobiography blends her life story with contemplation of the Gospels, and includes her divine visions, which allow her to interact with biblical figures, including Jesus. While this may sound strange to twenty-first-century ears, this brand of contemplation was encouraged for the devout by her religious tradition, and her divine visions gave her certain theological authority. What distinguished her work from her male contemporaries, however, was her "voice," or rather, "voices"—which include her "historical" voice, a third person narrator, and the character of Margery—within the stories. The result is what Glenn calls "*dialogism*, a conversation among conflicting intentions, values, claims, opinions—a conversation among her selves"

(108). Another distinguishing feature of Kempe's autobiography is its fragmented structure; she tells stories not in chronological order but in a "cyclical and associational [. . .] record of her spiritual development" (107). Indeed, these rhetorical strategies significantly depart from the unified voice and strict linear structure privileged by classical rhetoric.

Finally, Kempe's work, in its candidness and intimacy, is often challenging to cultural norms, narrating stories that reveal her desire to have a chaste relationship with her husband or to insist that even as a married layperson, she has the right to dress in white wool, as "the bride of Christ." Of her brazen rhetorical decisions, Glenn writes, "Perhaps only a woman (untrained in and unconscious of standard rhetorical and literary practices) would assert her *self* this way" (106).

Like Julian of Norwich, Kempe's words were not heard in her lifetime. Her text was preserved, but neglected, until 1934 and eventually published in 1940. When her words were finally made audible, scholars called the structure illogical and incoherent and accused Kempe of hysteria—particularly because some of her visions emerged postpartum. In this way, her femaleness became a liability; her female body (and hormones) was thought to taint her mind. Feminist rhetors, on the other hand, hear her voice differently, as introducing "unprecedented artistic and rhetorical techniques" and feminizing Christianity (104).

Together, Julian of Norwich and Margery Kempe both argued for and enacted women's participation in Christianity. Their rhetoric also altered theological discourse, blending personal story and scripture and, particularly in the case of Julian, writing to an audience of presumed equals. In the work of Julian of Norwich and Margery Kempe, then, we find early examples of the insistence by feminist rhetors that "the personal" is a legitimate site for knowledge, and that the stories of those who are culturally marginalized can serve to disrupt and change dominant discourse.

For Writing and Discussion

1. Do a Google search for current news about the role of women in contemporary Christianity. What strategies do contemporary women use to complicate, challenge, and speak back to church doctrine? How do these connect to or diverge from those used by Julian of Norwich or Margery Kempe?

2. Whereas Cheryl Glenn reads Kempe's use of multiple voices and "associational" structure as a rhetorical choice with its own logic, some of the scholars who read it after its initial publication called it illogical and incoherent—terms often applied to women, themselves. In what ways does the dualism of male/logical or female/illogical still linger in our culture? How do these connotations shape our assumptions about good writing?

LOCATING WOMEN'S RHETORICAL CHALLENGES TO FEMININITY

In addition to challenging church doctrine, feminist rhetors have also recovered the voices of women who made some of the first public arguments for women's intellectual participation in society. From these recovered voices, we learn how those who have been excluded from a discourse find ways to both enter and to disrupt it. Because their most likely audience was men, these writers often had to make their arguments quite strategically, assuaging potential fears of male readers at the same time that they challenged the patriarchal status quo.

The earliest example of this may well be Christine de Pizan (1365–1430), the first woman to support herself by writing. In *The Book of the City of Ladies*, de Pizan draws upon fictional (or some would say, mythical) visits from three ladies—Lady Reason, Lady Rectitude, and Lady Justice—who help her to challenge misogynist depictions of women, and instead to argue that the subjugation of women prevents an ideal society (Ritchie and Ronald 32). Therefore, she argues, women should be allowed education and speech so as to contribute to the betterment of their communities and culture.

This argument that realizing women's full humanity, by allowing them education and public participation, would facilitate larger societal ideals is one other female rhetors employed to their advantage, as well. We see this in the writing of Mary Astell, who wrote almost three hundred years after de Pizan. Astell was born in England in 1666 and was educated by her uncle, an Anglican priest. Instead of marrying, Astell moved to London to write. She published books and pamphlets, the most notable being *A Serious Proposal to Ladies: Parts I and II* (1694), in which she argues for a "Religious Retirement," which would allow women like herself, who did not marry, to serve the community and to benefit from intellectual dialogue among women.

Unlike some of her fellow female writers, Astell received public praise for her work, which may be attributed to her able use of classical rhetorical skills as well as to what Christine Mason Sutherland calls her obvious "study of her audience," which allowed her to aptly appeal to her readers' interests (99). For instance, as a woman writing during a time when female speech was equated with female impurity, she directly addressed this potential concern by contending that training of the female mind would aid control of passions and therefore promote morality. So while she doesn't go so far as to challenge cultural notions of morality, she disrupts the idea that a speaking woman is an immoral woman and insists that women have a natural right to education.

While Astell was viewed as a rhetor that succeeded within the strictures of traditional rhetoric, her textual practices altered it, as well. Rather than abide by the tradition of classical rhetoric to emphasize opposition and verbal victory, she promotes collective search for truth. In her words, "we pervert Reason when we make it the Instrument of an Endless Contention" (*Serious Proposal: Part II* 162). In this way, she served as a predecessor to feminist rhetors and teachers, who later complicate notions of argument as a two-sided, either/or debate, with the primary goal of changing the "opponent's" mind.

About 150 years later, another writer, Margaret Fuller (1810–1850), also challenged traditional forms of argument in her landmark manifesto *Woman in the Nineteenth Century* (1845), which likely served as one impetus for the Seneca Falls Convention, an important gathering to advocate for women's rights as US citizens. Fuller was born in Massachusetts, and she worked as a professional writer in many capacities: poet, travel writer, literary critic, editor of the literary journal *The Dial*, and journalist. Fuller cofounded *The Dial* with Ralph Waldo Emerson and shared an intellectual community with other male Transcendentalists. She was a strong advocate for women's participation in public and intellectual life, and in 1839 she introduced "Conversations," regular gatherings of women in her Boston home, which would allow them "time, patience, mutual reverence and fearlessness eno' to get at one another's thoughts" (qtd. in Kolodny 150). Together, the women discussed philosophy, literature, and politics, and it was this multivoiced mode of dialogue that Fuller aimed to replicate in her writing.

Fuller's work represents deep investment in inquiry, for it is through this process of investigation that she believed "truth" (in this case the notion that women deserve full participation in society) would follow.

This meant making room for conflicting views, so her writing includes a range of voices, forms, and positions; for instance, she melds her own argument with a speech by John Quincy Adams, an essay by French writer Susanne Necker, poetry by Transcendentalist William Ellery Channing, and a recording of mythological and historical events. As she writes, the goal is not to locate "ourselves at once on either side" but to "look upon the subject from the best point of view" (20).

While some criticized her text for haphazardly collecting voices or merely reflecting in print "uncontrolled female talkativeness" (Kolodny 160), feminist readings help us to hear her voice differently. They read her nonlinear, multivoiced text as a refusal to abide by authoritarian notions of persuasion and instead to write as a facilitator of dialogue and inquiry. While her male contemporaries like Emerson touted self-examination and self-reliance, Fuller sought to establish a collaborative dialogue that makes room for women to "search their own experience and intuitions" as well as to collectively discover new possibilities for women's experience of full humanity (vi). In this way, we can read Fuller as an early advocate for practices upon which later feminist writers would build their work, including collaborative inquiry and multi-genre texts.

For Writing and Discussion

1. Each of the writers discussed above appealed to her audience by insisting that enlarging the scope of women's rights would, in turn, benefit society as it existed. That is, they argued that the addition of women's rights would improve, but not challenge, the status quo. What are current examples of groups or individuals using a similar tact to advocate for improved conditions in their own lives? What are the limits and possibilities of such an approach?

2. Find an example of a speaker or writer making an argument to an audience who is likely opposed to his or her message. What strategies does the speaker/writer employ? Does the speaker/writer try to appease and challenge? How effective do you judge the argument? Why?

LOCATING A PUBLIC VOICE: THE RHETORIC OF THE SUFFRAGISTS AND ABOLITIONISTS

The suffragists are often considered the foremothers of the women's movement because of their deliberate, organized efforts to mobilize on behalf of women's rights. Given their overt public advocacy, it isn't surprising that these women were also among the first to be recovered as part of the rhetorical tradition. In fact, Karlyn Kohrs Campbell's 1989 two-volume collection of "great women speakers," *Man Cannot Speak for Her,* which features women's public speeches from 1832 to 1920, was one of the first major contributions to the feminist rhetorical project.

While women like Elizabeth Cady Stanton, Susan B. Anthony, and Sojourner Truth are often given brief lip service in recounts of US history as organizers or social activists, adding them to the rhetorical tradition means listening differently to the way they crafted and delivered their arguments in order to be heard. For instance, when Anthony was tried in court in 1873 for voting as a woman, she had to continually battle the judge's attempts to silence her. Anthony ignored the judge's repeated commands that she sit down and stop speaking; instead, she spoke at length (despite his interruptions) to convince the judge that the Constitution's granting the "citizen's right to vote" should include women and to remind him that laws are "interpreted by men, in favor of men, and against women" ("From" 155). Like women before her who reinterpreted the Bible to emphasize women's worth in God's eyes, Anthony reinterpreted the US Constitution to include women as citizens deserving of the right to vote. The judge was not convinced of her argument and ultimately fined her. Even so, she retorted, "I shall never pay a dollar of your unjust penalty," firmly maintaining her own boundaries of justice. The fact that Anthony had to struggle not only for the right to vote but also for the right to speak in court underscores Ritchie and Ronald's point that women rhetors across history "must first invent a way to speak in the context of being silenced and rendered invisible as persons" (xvii). Anthony would not stand for either injustice.

As familiar as Susan B. Anthony's name, so too is the phrase, "Ain't I a Woman?" It may not be as well known, however, that the line comes from an 1851 speech by Sojourner Truth, a freed slave, delivered at a Woman's Rights Convention in Ohio. The speech is built upon

Truth's powerful, charging voice, which she used to insist that despite falling outside of traditional femininity and despite being subjugated to slavery, "Aren't I a woman?"[1] "I could work as much and eat a much as a man (when I could get it), and bear the lash as well—and aren't I a woman? I have borne thirteen children and seen them almost all sold off to slavery, and when I cried out with a mother's grief, none but Jesus heard—and aren't I a woman?" (145). According to the transcription of the speech, "she bared her right arm to the shoulder, showing her tremendous muscular power" (145), an act that ties her body to her words, reminding the listeners that "woman" is not a singular category. She argues, with her words and body, that womanhood does not belong to only those who exemplify traditional notions of femininity. "The man over there says that women need to be helped into carriages, and lifted over ditches, and to have the best place everywhere. Nobody ever helps me into carriages, or over mud puddles, or gives me any best place [. . .] and aren't I a woman?" (144 –45). The act of evoking her body to support her argument provides a striking contrast to masculinist rhetoric that divides the intellect of the mind from the presumed irrationalism of the body.

Of course, even Truth's act of speech in this setting—a women's rights convention dominated by white women—was considered exceptional. She could not read or write, so Frances Gage, a white woman who presided over the convention, transcribed it. The fact that we hear Truth's voice through the words of a white woman raises questions akin to those that surround Aspasia, whom we hear through men. How, we might wonder, have her words have been changed or appropriated? The complexity surrounding Truth's voice, words, and body also requires us to think about the relationship between white women and black women in the struggle for women's rights—a struggle from which black women were largely excluded. Even as questions remain about the speech's authenticity, it remains, as Ritchie and Ronald argue, "one of the most important documents in both feminist and women's rhetorical history" because the words assigned to Truth "broke open" what it meant to be a woman at this historical moment (144).

In addition to recovering the voices of women whose names may evoke historical recognition, feminist scholars have also illuminated the work of rhetors that have long been historically marginalized or silenced. One such figure is Ida B. Wells, who was not recognized for her profound public challenges against racism and sexism until the

Chapter 2: The Rhetorical Tradition Through a Feminist Lens   33

late twentieth century. Wells was born a slave in 1862 and, following emancipation, moved to Memphis, Tennessee, where she became the editor of the *Evening Star*, a nationally syndicated columnist, a public speaker, and an activist. She is perhaps best known for her journalistic response to the lynching of three men, one who was a close friend, in 1892. This incident led her to make a fiery charge against lynching, which she came to understand as "an instrument used to retard the progress of African Americans in their efforts to participate more fully in social, political and economic life" (Royster 170).

As Jacqueline Jones Royster points out, Wells followed the African American female tradition of using whatever literacy skills she possessed to speak out against injustice, and above all, to tell the truth simply and directly. After the lynching of these three men, whom she knew and respected, she began what we would now call investigative reporting, researching and documenting other incidents of lynching. In one editorial, she told a truth that so angered white members of the Memphis community, they did everything they could to silence her. She wrote:

> Eight negroes lynched in one week. [. . .] The same program of hanging then shooting bullets into the lifeless bodies was carried out to the letter. Nobody in this section of the country believes the old threadbare lie that negro men rape white women. If Southern white men are not careful they will overreach themselves, and public sentiment will have a reaction. A conclusion will then be reached which will be very damaging to the moral reputation of their women. (195)

After the piece was published, the press was destroyed, death threats were issued against her partner, and Wells was warned that if she returned to Memphis, she would be killed. She moved to New York, where she could continue her writing. In her autobiography, Wells writes, "[I] owed it to myself and to my race to tell the whole truth" (qtd. in Royster 171).

In her subsequent editorial "Lynch Law in All its Phases" (1893), Wells describes in exacting detail the events leading to the 1892 lynching as well as the harrowing experience of those left behind: "The baby daughter of Tom Moss [one of the men lynched], too young to express how she misses her father, toddles to the wardrobe, seizes the legs of the trousers of his letter-carrier uniform, hugs and kisses them with evident delight and stretches up her little hands to be taken up into the arms which will nevermore clasp his daughter's form" (193). With these words, she humanizes Moss, connecting the brutal and inhumane lynching to a man, a father. Wells wisely highlights a shared set of patriotic values with her readers, suggesting that these unjust attacks, which shake the very foundation of liberty on which America is built, must not be known to her readers—otherwise they would not have allowed them. She writes: "I am before the American people today through no inclination of my own, but because of a deep-seated conviction that the country at large does not know the extent to which lynch law prevails in parts of the Republic, nor the conditions which force into exile those who speak the truth" (189–90). Her writing, then, aims to correct this ignorance and to insist that her readers must prevent lynchings, not only to protect African Americans but also to "preserve our institutions" (190).

These last examples demonstrate that while some women wrote to establish "rooms of their own," to quote Virginia Woolf, others wrote to survive. By considering the range of purposes and contexts that informed women's writing, it becomes clear that any definition of women's rhetoric has to be multiple, flexible, and expansive.

In the next chapter, I continue to offer examples of the changing face, sound, and scope of the rhetorical tradition as a result of feminist contributions. Rather than focus on key figures, as I have done here, I show how feminist contributions grew from these first, singular voices into a proliferation of speech acts that brought to light issues of diversity and difference, disrupted traditional rhetorical forms, and expanded what constitutes rhetorical contexts.

For Writing and Discussion

1. What is gained from approaching someone like Susan B. Anthony or Sojourner Truth as a rhetor—someone who engages in argument for social change—as well as an activist, historical icon, etc.?

2. When you consider the historical, cultural contexts that shaped the arguments of rhetors like Anthony, Truth, and Ida B. Wells, what made their strategies particularly effective within that situation?

Works Cited

Aspasia. "'Pericles' Funeral Oration' from Plato's *Menexenus*." *Available Means: An Anthology of Women's Rhetoric(s)*. Ed. Joy Ritchie and Kate Ronald. Pittsburgh, PA: U of Pittsburgh P, 2001. 2–8. Print.

Astell, Mary. *A Serious Proposal to the Ladies: Parts I and II*. London: Broadview, 2002. Print.

Berlin, James. *Rhetoric and Reality: Writing Instruction in American Colleges, 1900–1985*. Carbondale: Southern Illinois UP, 1987. Print.

Bizzell, Patricia. "The Intellectual Work of 'Mixed' Forms of Academic Discourse." *Alt Dis: Alternative Discourses and the Academy*. Ed. Christopher Schroeder, Helen Fox, and Patricia Bizzell. Portsmouth, NH: Heinemann, 2002. 1–10. Print.

Campbell, Karlyn Kohrs. *Man Cannot Speak for Her, Volume I: A Critical Study of Early Feminist Rhetoric*. New York: Greenwood Press, 1989. Print.

—. *Man Cannot Speak for Her, Volume II: Key Texts of the Early Feminists*. New York: Greenwood Press, 1989. Print.

Connors, Robert J. *Composition-Rhetoric: Backgrounds, Theory, and Pedagogy*. Pittsburgh, PA: U of Pittsburgh P, 1997. Print.

Corbett, Edward P. J. *Classical Rhetoric for the Modern Student*. New York: Oxford UP, 1971. Print.

de Pizan, Christine. *The Book of the City of Ladies*. Trans. Rosalind Brown-Grant. New York: Penguin, 2000. Print.

Diotima. "'On Love' from Plato's *Symposium*." *Available Means: An Anthology of Women's Rhetoric(s)*. Ed. Joy Ritchie and Kate Ronald. Pittsburgh, PA: U of Pittsburgh P, 2001. 10–15. Print.

"From *The United States of America v. Susan B. Anthony (1873)*." *Available Means: An Anthology of Women's Rhetoric(s)*. Ed. Joy Ritchie and Kate Ronald. Pittsburgh, PA: U of Pittsburgh P, 2001. 152–56. Print.

Fuller, Margaret. *Woman in the Nineteenth Century*. Mineola, New York: Dover, 1999. Print.

Glenn, Cheryl. *Rhetoric Retold: Regendering the Tradition from Antiquity Through the Renaissance*. Carbondale: Southern Illinois UP, 1997. Print.

Golden, James L., Goodwin F. Berquist, and William E. Coleman. *The Rhetoric of Western Thought*. 5th ed. Dubuque, IA: Kendall/Hunt Publishing Company, 1993. Print.

Jarratt, Susan C. *Rereading the Sophists: Classical Rhetoric Refigured*. Carbondale: Southern Illinois UP, 1998. Print.

Jarratt, Susan, and Rory Ong. "Aspasia: Rhetoric, Gender, and Colonial Ideology." *Reclaiming Rhetorica: Women in the Rhetorical Tradition*. Ed. Andrea A. Lunsford. Pittsburgh, PA: U of Pittsburgh P, 1995. 9–24. Print.

Julian of Norwich. *Revelations of Divine Love*. Trans. Elizabeth Spearing. London: Penguin Classics, 1998. Print.

Kempe, Margery. *The Book of Margery Kempe*. Trans. John Skinner. New York: Random House, 1998. Print.
Kolodny, Annette. "Inventing a Feminist Discourse: Rhetoric and Resistance in Margaret Fuller's *Woman in the Nineteenth Century*." *Reclaiming Rhetorica: Women in the Rhetorical Tradition*. Ed. Andrea A. Lunsford. Pittsburgh, PA: U of Pittsburgh P, 1995. 137–66. Print.
Loraux, Nicole. *The Children of Athena*. Trans. Caroline Levine. Princeton, NJ: Princeton UP, 1993. Print.
Ritchie, Joy, and Kate Ronald. *Available Means: An Anthology of Women's Rhetoric(s)*. Pittsburgh, PA: U of Pittsburgh P, 2001. Print.
Royster, Jacqueline Jones. "To Call a Thing by Its True Name: The Rhetoric of Ida B. Wells." *Reclaiming Rhetorica: Women in the Rhetorical Tradition*. Ed. Andrea A. Lunsford. Pittsburgh, PA: U of Pittsburgh P, 1995. 167–84. Print.
Sutherland, Christine Mason. "Mary Astell: Reclaiming Rhetorica in the Seventeenth Century." *Reclaiming Rhetorica: Women in the Rhetorical Tradition*. Ed. Andrea A. Lunsford. Pittsburgh, PA: U of Pittsburgh P, 1995. 93–116. Print.
Swearingen, C. Jan. "A Lover's Discourse: Diotima, Logos, and Desire." *Reclaiming Rhetorica: Women in the Rhetorical Tradition*. Ed. Andrea A. Lunsford. Pittsburgh, PA: U of Pittsburgh P, 1995. 25–52. Print.
Truth, Sojourner. "Speech at the Woman's Rights Convention, Akron Ohio." *Available Means: An Anthology of Women's Rhetoric(s)*. Ed. Joy Ritchie and Kate Ronald. Pittsburgh, PA: U of Pittsburgh P, 2001. 144–45. Print.
Wells, Ida B. "Lynch Law in All its Phases." *Available Means: An Anthology of Women's Rhetoric(s)*. Ed. Joy Ritchie and Kate Ronald. Pittsburgh, PA: U of Pittsburgh P, 2001. 189–203. Print.

For Further Reading

Carlson, Cheree A. "Aspasia of Miletus: How One Woman Disappeared from the History of Rhetoric." *Women's Studies in Communication* 17.1 (1994): 26–44. Print.
Donawerth, Jane. "Poaching on Men's Philosophies of Rhetoric: Eighteenth- and Nineteenth-Century Rhetorical Theory by Women." *Philosophy and Rhetoric* 33.3 (2000): 243–58. Print.
Eldred, Janet Carey, and Peter Mortensen. *Imagining Rhetoric: Composing Women of the Early United States*. Pittsburgh, PA: U of Pittsburgh, 2002. Print.
Jarratt, Susan C. *Rereading the Sophists: Classical Rhetoric Refigured*. Carbondale: Southern Illinois UP, 1991. Print.

Kienzle, Beverly Mayne, and Pamela J. Walker. *Women Preachers and Prophets through Two Millennia of Christianity*. Berkeley: U of California, 1998. Print.

Schiappa, Edward. *Landmark Essays on Classical Greek Rhetoric*. Davis, CA: Hermagoras, 1994. Print.

Wertheimer, Molly Meijer. *Listening to Their Voices: The Rhetorical Activities of Historical Women*. Columbia: U of South Carolina, 1997. Print.

3 Difference, Form, and Topoi Through a Feminist Lens

The first "wave" of recovered women's voices proved that the rhetorical tradition was not absent female voices; women's voices were simply unheard or discounted. As Kacey, a student in my Rhetoric of Women Writers class wisely noted, "If there's any common theme that I've learned from [women's rhetoric] so far, it's that silence is not an absence." Indeed, what we long assumed to be silence was really a lack of listening to and for women's voices.

The presence of rhetors like Aspasia, Margery Kempe, and Susan B. Anthony in the rhetorical tradition reminds us that women have used their intellect, resources, and courage to contribute to public discourse and to challenge societal constructions of women throughout history. Additionally, their inclusion alters the rhetorical tradition's reputation as, to quote Quintilian, "good men speaking well." Not only do they insist that women can occupy the category of rhetor but they also extend what counts as "speaking [and writing] well"—and their expanded ideas of speech, knowledge, and inquiry influence writing instruction in classrooms today.

As important as these examples of powerful voices are, however, the recovery of individual figures tends to emphasize women who were in some way exceptional. This is not to disregard either the work of these women rhetors, who were indeed heroic in their bravery, determination, and acumen, or the crucial work employed by feminist scholars to recover them; but as feminist scholars like Joy Ritchie and Kate Ronald have argued, "the method of 'recovering' women's rhetoric by describing isolated incidents of one or two brilliant, brave (and often white and privileged) women somehow gaining a platform through sheer will or inspiration keeps the 'recurrences' or the 'traces' of the emerging tradition [in women's rhetoric] invisible" (xix). That is, it keeps the focus on exceptional individuals rather than on rhetorical patterns that emerged among communities of women rhetors and as women borrowed rhetorical strategies from one another.

However, as feminist scholars devoted increasing attention to feminist rhetoric, the range and directions of scholarly pursuits also began to flourish. Subsequently, the diversity of voices and forms represented in the rhetorical tradition and the distinct rhetorical contributions offered by women became more discernable. Ritchie and Ronald's *Available Means: An Anthology of Women's Rhetoric(s)*, the most expansive collection of women's rhetoric to date, is one such example. The collection includes seventy women's voices from Aspasia to Audre Lorde to Toni Morrison, and it also comprises writers who "have not been heard in any tradition" (xxi). The collection further expands the forms and the rhetorical contexts represented by women's rhetoric. For instance, *Available Means* includes writers who wrote in forms that are not usually valued as rhetorical, like letters, journals, or meditations, and based in contexts never considered in the rhetorical tradition, like the kitchen, the nursery, the parlor, the garden. In addition to *Available Means* came rich studies of particular groups of women rhetors—including Shirley Wilson Logan's *"We are Coming": The Persuasive Discourse of Nineteenth Century Black Women*, Jacqueline Jones Royster's *Traces of a Stream: Literacy and Social Change Among African American Women*, and Anne Ruggles Gere's *Intimate Practices: Literacy and Cultural Work in U.S. Women's Clubs, 1880–1920*—which help to demonstrate patterns of recurrent themes and connective threads among women's rhetorics. Taken together, these texts show what we can learn from studying how women's communities have borrowed and shared rhetorical strategies. They also illuminate the convergences and divergences that result from women writers' differences in race, class, sexual identity, or geographical location.

In what follows, I focus on three key issues featured in contemporary feminist rhetorical projects. They include attention to difference and diversity; new rhetorical forms and strategies; and new rhetorical topoi, or the topics and places from which arguments can be made. Not only did these contributions expand rhetorical studies, but they also extended the kind of texts students could study, discuss, and compose in composition classrooms.

Acknowledging Difference among Women

The phrase a "room of her own" is probably as famous as Virginia Woolf is, herself. Indeed, Woolf's book *A Room of One's Own* (1929) serves as a significant historical touchstone for feminist writers and rhetoricians. In this text, Woolf launched the memorable argument that a woman who wants to write needs a room of her own and money to support herself. While her insistence of women's need for space, resources, and time to assert their own voices was indeed radical at the time, it did not necessarily take into account the material realities of most women's lives. As African American writer Alice Walker would later ask, what about the slave women, who owned not even themselves? How could she conceive of a room of her own?

For Woolf it is a phantom that impedes her creative work—The Angel in the House, who is charming, unselfish, and successful in all elements of "family life." She is deeply self-sacrificing, with not a "mind or a wish of her own" (243). The Angel represents idealized notions of femininity that school women to believe that women's identities are dependent upon serving others' needs, not in defining and realizing their own. To be sure, efforts to be The Angel foreclosed possibilities for being a writer.

What is Woolf's response to The Angel? "It was she who bothered me and wasted my time and so tormented me," she writes, "that at last I killed her" (243). When my students and I read this excerpt from Woolf's *A Room of One's Own*, they are struck by how many of these traits are still expected of women—by how pressured women still feel as students, as writers, as scholars, as well as in their personal lives, to emulate The Angel. Yet we also must ask, "Who can kill The Angel?" For which women is it easier to reject this notion of femininity?

Writing in 1971 Adrienne Rich, poet, essayist, professor, and rhetorician, reminds readers that Woolf addressed the situation for one group of women—those who were economically and racially privileged—but left out "women who are washing other people's dishes and caring for other people's children, not to mention women who went on the streets last night in order to feed their children" (272). In other words, Rich calls attention to the women who had no choice but to assume the role of the self-sacrificing Angel—and often The Angel in another woman's house, not her own—when white, wealthy women refused that role.

I focus on Woolf's piece and on subsequent responses because it exemplifies how the women's movement (and feminist rhetorical work) emerged from powerful and important voices, but these voices did not always reflect the diversity of experience, roles, and complexities of women's lives. Consequently, new voices entered the dialogue to offer a richer picture of womanhood, women's rhetoric, and the feminist movement. Referring to how this process ensued in English studies, Rich writes:

> without a growing feminist movement, the first inroads of feminist scholarship could not have been made; without the sharpening of black feminist consciousness, black women's writing would have been left in limbo between misogynist black male critics and white feminists still struggling to unearth a white women's tradition; without an articulate lesbian/feminist movement, lesbian writing would still be lying in that closet where many of us used to sit reading forbidden books "in a bad light." (269)

Of course, this move toward embracing difference was not—is not—smooth or easy. Speaking at an academic conference in 1979 where she was one of very few participants of color, Audre Lorde, a black, lesbian poet and essayist, called attention to the necessity of moving beyond a mere "tolerance of difference," which she called "the grossest of reformism." Instead, she argues, we must view difference as a resource, "a fund of necessary polarities between which our creativity can spark like a dialectic" (111). On this occasion and many others, Lorde challenged white women and women of color to examine the social and material differences that exist among them so that they could come together to affect change.

As feminism grew and developed, so too did its attention to identity as multiple, fluid, and often contradictory—something that cannot be separated from social, economic, and historical contexts. Consequently, singular identity categories like race or sexuality began to shift to an emphasis on what Minnie Bruce Pratt, in 1995, called "the complexities of woman" (431). Writing from her complex social location as a white, once-married, now lesbian, feminine-looking, mother, partner, poet, and teacher, she challenges rigid, uniform categories of gender and sexuality. She writes:

> Here I still stand, unmistakably "feminine" in style, and "womanly" in personal experience—and unacceptably "masculine" in political interests and in my dedication to writing poetry that stretches beyond the woman's domain of home. Here I am, assigned a "female" sex on my birth certificate, but not considered womanly enough—because I am a lesbian—to retain custody of the children I delivered from my woman's body. (432)

In addition to attending to interlocking categories of race, class, gender, and sexuality, Gloria Anzaldúa, a Chicana poet, theorist, and essayist, reminds us of another important contributor to identity: language. Anzaldúa describes a life lived on the border of Texas and Mexico, of Spanish and English: "I remember being caught speaking Spanish at recess—that was good for three licks on the knuckles with a sharp ruler. [. . .] If you want to be American, speak 'American.' If you don't like it, go back to Mexico where you belong" (53). She goes on to explain that difference is not confined to dualisms: English or Spanish; Mexican or American; male or female; gay or straight. Chicanos, she writes, are a "complex, heterogeneous people," who speak many languages, including standard English, working class and slang English, Standard Spanish, Standard Mexican Spanish, North Mexican Spanish dialect, Chicano Spanish, Tex-Mex, and *Pachuco* (a secret language of rebellion) (359). To accept herself, she argues, she must accept as legitimate all of these languages: "Ethnic identity is twin skin to linguistic identity—I am my language" (59).

Because the deep connection between language and identity has played a strong role in the composition classroom—think back, for instance, to late nineteenth-century Harvard, where students' poor writing indicated deficient character—it is probably not surprising that Anzaldúa's essays are often included in first-year composition readers. Indeed, beginning in the 1960s, and most notably articulated in the 1974 statement "Students' Right to Their Own Language," the field of Composition Studies has sought to challenge singular ideas of a "standard" English and to encourage teachers to validate students' home languages. Anzaldúa's piece provides a powerful public example of what is gained by viewing linguistic diversity as a resource, not a problem.

Chapter 3: Difference, Form, and Topoi Through a Feminist Lens   43

While writers like Walker, Lorde, Rich, Pratt, and Anzaldúa were already renowned contributors to feminist creative and critical work, their voices enrich the rhetorical tradition by illuminating the ways difference informs one's "available means" to speak, to be heard, and to represent oneself. These rhetors also challenge singular notions of womanhood, while exposing the power differentials that affect women's relationships to one another and to the larger culture. In the next section, I consider the rhetorical strategies they employ to do this work, insisting on the dialectical relationship of form and content and the way in which form, itself, makes meaning.

FOR WRITING AND DISCUSSION

1. By informally interviewing faculty or researching curricular documents (course catalogues, major requirements, etc.), trace how the presence of women's writing emerged in your own department. Who were the first writers taught? Why? To what extent are women currently represented within the undergraduate and/or graduate curriculum? How is difference among women represented?

2. Take a look at the document "Students' Right to Their Own Language," which can be found at: http://www.ncte.org/library/NCTEFiles/Groups/CCCC/NewSRTOL.pdf. Where do you stand in relation to this position statement? Why? Did you see these principles reflected in your education?

REJECTING THE MASTER'S TOOLS

In one of her best known essays, Audre Lorde contends, *"the master's tools will never dismantle the master's house.* They may allow us to temporarily beat him at his own game, but they will never enable us to bring about genuine change" (112). As I showed in the last chapter, women rhetors have long sought to both work within and against the "master's" discourse—to cushion and appease at the same time they challenge and disrupt. Lorde, writing in the 1970s, urged women to cease defining the "master's house" as their only source of support or resource of knowledge (112). Instead, she argues that women need to *"reach down into that deep place of knowledge inside* [themselves]," which she sees as a way for (particularly white) women to become accountable for privilege and confront their fears of difference. "Then," she writes, "the personal as the political can begin to illuminate all our choices" (113). Indeed, this was an historical moment when many feminists echoed the call for women to develop new forms through which to argue, question, and inquire, and in so doing, to denaturalize the seemingly "universal" rhetorical standards of clear, linear, logical prose. It is probably not surprising, then, that an important strategy for women writing during what is commonly called the "second wave"[2] of the feminist movement was to embrace and reclaim the feminine, including a feminine mode of writing.

Hélène Cixous, French feminist and theorist, offers one of the most renowned examples of this effort in her 1975 theory of *ecriture* feminine, the practice of writing through female experience—reclaiming the female voice by writing "from" the female body. For Cixous, writing as woman necessarily differs from writing according to the codes of masculinist conventions. "Her discourse, even when 'theoretical' or political," Cixous writes, "is never simple or linear or 'objectivized,' universalized; she involves her whole story in history" (285). Within traditional rhetoric, Cixous argues, "The orator is asked to unwind a thin thread, dry and taut" (285). Indeed, if we look to the way Edward P. J. Corbett has translated classical rhetoric for students, we see an emphasis on a predetermined argument that can be unwound without deviations or departures from the plan. He writes, "The beginning of all good writing is a sharply defined subject. [. . .] it would be futile to start inscribing words on a blank sheet of paper without having carefully plotted one's direction and destination" (38). Cixous contends that women, on the other hand, "like uneasiness, questioning. There is waste in what we say. We need that waste" (285). Referring simultaneously to the female voice and the female body, which she sees as intimately connected, Cixous embraces what is typically deemed "excess"—words, digressions, flesh, waste. She writes:

> We have turned away from our bodies. Shamefully we have been taught to be unaware of them, to lash them with stupid modesty; we've been tricked into a fool's bargain: each one is to love the other sex. I'll give you your body and you will give me men. But which men give women the body that they blindly hand over to him? Why so few texts? Because there are still so few

women winning back their bodies. Woman must write her body, must make up the unimpeded tongue that bursts partitions, classes, and rhetorics, orders and codes, must inundate, run through, go beyond the discourse with its last reserves, including the one of laughing off the word "silence" that has to be said, the one that, aiming for the impossible, stops dead before the word "impossible" and writes it as "end." (287)

Indeed, this adoption of writing strategies that exceed normative conventions might well be considered part of the feminist rhetorical tradition—something we see in writing dating back to (and probably before) Margery Kempe; Cixous's overtly articulated and brazen disruption of these standards, however, established deeper inroads for other feminist writers to follow. For instance, Cixous's influence can be felt in the work of Trinh T. Minh-ha, a Vietnamese feminist writer, filmmaker, and composer, who writes over a decade later. She, too, illuminates the oft-unchallenged discursive norm, explaining, "*Clear* expression, often equated with *correct* expression, has long been the criterion set forth in treatises on *rhetoric*, whose aim was to order discourse so as to *persuade*" (16). Rather than tying this notion of clarity (only) to gender, she shows how it is connected to western culture. Consequently, the language of eastern philosophy, such as Taoism and Zen, "which is perfectly accessible but rife with paradox," is not considered clear writing according to western thought, because paradox is often considered "illogical" or "nonsensical," and the point of this writing is not to persuade (16).

Reflective of the historical moment in which each wrote, Cixous highlights gender difference to the detriment of other kinds of difference (in fact, she was later critiqued for essentializing gender and ignoring difference), while Trinh[3] explores the way multiple social and cultural factors shape assumptions about language and identity. Even so, both come to a similar argument about masculine discourse: By excising language not deemed "clear," we also lose out on alternative ways of knowing, writing, and living. While Aristotle contends, "Language which does not convey a clear meaning fails to perform the very function of language," Trinh offers an alternative perspective: "To write 'clearly,' one must incessantly prune, eliminate, forbid, purge, purify" (17).

Both Cixous and Trinh also move beyond an argument for new discursive possibilities to enact them. Cixous melds linguistic argument with images and metaphors of the female body, resisting linearity, and engaging in "sarcasm, word-play, lyricism, and exhortation" (Ritchie and Ronald 284). Trinh merges writers and thinkers from multiple disciplines, creating compelling juxtapositions and layers of language and images (she also includes photographs), rather than building to a unified, coherent point. She blends the poetic and theoretical, storytelling and argument. As you might recall, some of these strategies hark back (though perhaps not intentionally) to those employed by writers like Mary Astell, who aimed in her prose for inquiry rather than victory in a two-sided debate, or Margaret Fuller, who offered a range of voices in her text so as to provide readers a multifaceted lens through which to see an issue.

One of the central projects of feminist rhetoric is to include and value in writing that which conventional norms have traditionally disregarded. As I show above, this has meant including writing that emerges from the feminine self, the body, as well as composing in forms that do not follow a linear, "rational" form. Anzaldúa offers another important contribution to form-as-argument, as she melds not only poetry and prose but also Spanish (in multiple forms) and English. That is, her writing enacts the borderland she describes, showing what is made possible by dwelling in the "in-between" space of cultures and languages, sexual, racial, class-based, and gender identities:

> As a *mestiza* I have no country, my homeland cast me out; yet all countries are mine because I am every woman's sister or potential lover. (As a lesbian I have no race, my own people disclaim me; but I am all races because there is the queer of me in all races.) I am cultureless because, as a feminist, I challenge the collective cultural/religious male-derived beliefs of Indo-Hispanics and Anglos; yet I am cultured because I am participating in the creation of yet another culture, a new story to explain the world and our participation in it, a new value system with images and symbols that connect us to each other and to the planet. *Soy un amasamiento*, I am an act of kneading, of uniting and joining that not only has produced both a creature of darkness and a creature

of light, but also a creature that questions the definitions of light and dark and gives them new meanings. (80–81)

Anzaldúa's text also exhibits a principled refusal to translate for English speakers, making explicit the ties between language and power. She writes, "Until I am free to write bilingually and to switch codes without always having to translate [. . .] as long as I have to accommodate the English speakers rather than having them accommodate me, my tongue will be illegitimate" (59). Again, her argument—and its enactment—speaks to larger, ongoing debates about composition instruction: To what extent should students be required to accommodate discursive norms in the academy? To what extent should teachers accommodate students' linguistic backgrounds? How must the university change as its student body becomes increasingly diverse?

While these writers use different strategies to complicate, critique, and extend masculinist language, perhaps the most commonly relied upon resource within feminist rhetoric is the use personal experience as a site of knowledge. Often deemed too subjective or "soft," the "I" is commonly forbidden from academic writing. Feminist writers, however, insist upon the legitimacy of the personal as a way to enhance and further knowledge. As Pratt writes, "we can not move theory into action unless we find it in the eccentric and wandering ways of our daily life. I have written [my stories] to give theory flesh and breath" (434).

FOR WRITING AND DISCUSSION

1. Read an excerpt by Hélène Cixous or Trinh T. Minh-ha (see Works Cited below). In what ways do their rhetorical choices disrupt what is typically deemed "conventional" writing? What is gained and lost through these choices?

2. Can you think of examples of scholarly texts you've read that include the "I" or a "personal" perspective on the subject at hand? What difference does this rhetorical choice make to your experience of the text?

Revising Rhetorical Contexts

In addition to expanding the diversity among voices, subjects, and forms reflected in rhetoric, feminist rhetors have also extended the boundaries of rhetorical contexts. Traditionally, rhetorical contexts have been defined as public spaces—scholarly lectures, political debates, religious sermons—sites from which women were historically excluded. Instead, then, women spoke and wrote out of the problems and concerns present in their own lives and locations. As a result of these new topoi—topics/places from which arguments emerge—women rhetors "expand the locus of rhetoric for all speakers and writers" (Ritchie and Ronald xxiii).

Ritchie and Ronald's collection includes texts from women who write out of their embodied experience, making issues of disability, breast cancer, and abuse worthy subjects of public discourse. Feminist rhetors have also conducted studies of women-centered sites to examine oft-devalued or ignored rhetorical forms and strategies employed by women. One such example is Gere's 1997 *Intimate Practices*, which culls from archival research a rich analysis of the cultural work performed by women's clubs. This work includes papers about immigrant assimilation, petitions drafted to support libraries or hospitals, programs providing topics for discussion and reading, as well as poems, plays, and magazines (2). Gere further shows how women involved in a range of group-defined clubs—including white working and middle-class, Mormon, Jewish, and African-American—used this space to define and refine their own identities. While this allowed for an affirmation of their womanhood, it often also resulted in exclusionary tactics—an issue that would not become a significant concern of the women's movement until much later. Ultimately, Gere's study emphasizes the range, depth, and cultural importance of work clubwomen conducted, a move that ultimately challenges stereotypes about communal spaces for women.

Beth Daniell's 2003 *A Communion of Friendship: Literacy, Spiritual Practice, and Women in Recovery* is another project that extends the realm of rhetorical contexts by examining the mainly private reading and writing practices of six women who participate in Al-Anon, all of whose husbands are alcoholics. As Daniell notes, her book challenges many entrenched ideas about literacy: that private literacy practices are not worthy of examination; that spiritual and emotional are not legitimate aspects of literacy; and that ordinary women's lives are not important enough to study and write about (2). While the women Daniell studies do not necessarily use literacy to make public arguments, Daniell shows that they use literacy "to make their lives more meaningful, no matter what their economic and political circumstances are" (6). Consequently, assumptions as to where rhetoric occurs and who produces it are challenged.

Gwendolyn D. Pough offers yet another example that disrupts the traditional topoi of rhetoric; her 2004 book, *Check It While I Wreck It: Black Womanhood, Hip-Hop Culture, and the Public Sphere*, shows how African-American women use rap to construct their own identities, give voice to their own experiences, and contribute to public dialogue on civil liberties, black womanhood, and rap, itself. Pough, then, not only illustrates how black female rappers appropriate and challenge a traditionally male (and sometimes misogynist) genre but also connects women's rap to a legacy of black women working for civil rights, dating all the way back to Sojourner Truth.

These are but a few examples of the growing body of work on women's rhetoric(s), which have altered the shape and sound of the rhetorical tradition. This scholarship on women's rhetoric(s) continues to expand, reminding us to value the local alongside the global, through studies of transnational women's rhetoric, and the diary and recipe, alongside explorations of feminist rhetoric in the digital age. Underscoring all feminist scholarship, however, is the tenet that subjectivity—that is, the complex, multiple cultural locations and positions that shape our experience of self—matters; the personal is political.

In part two of this book, I focus more explicitly on feminist contributions to composition classrooms and the teachers and students who animate them. The next chapter offers a look at how feminists have revised conceptions of the writing teacher and student. The two chapters that follow show how feminists have revised notions of research and the researcher, and how we conceive and deploy academic argument.

Works Cited

Anzaldúa, Gloria. *Borderlands/La Frontera: The New Mestiza*. San Francisco, CA: Aunt Lute Books, 1987. Print.

Cixous, Hélène. "Sorties." *Available Means: An Anthology of Women's Rhetoric(s)*. Ed. Joy Ritchie and Kate Ronald. Pittsburgh, PA: U of Pittsburgh P, 2001. 284–90. Print.

Corbett, Edward P. J. *Classical Rhetoric for the Modern Student.* New York: Oxford UP, 1971. Print.

Daniell, Beth. *A Communion of Friendship: Literacy, Spiritual Practice, and Women in Recovery.* Carbondale: Southern Illinois UP, 2003.

Gere, Anne Ruggles. *Intimate Practices: Literacy and Cultural Work in U.S. Women's Clubs: 1880–1920.* Urbana: U of Illinois P, 1997. Print.

Logan, Shirley Wilson. *"We are Coming": The Persuasive Discourse of Nineteenth Century Black Women.* Carbondale: Southern Illinois UP, 1999. Print.

Lord, Audre. *Sister Outsider.* Freedom, CA: The Crossing Press, 1984. Print.

Pough, Gwendolyn D. *Check It While I Wreck It: Black Womanhood, Hip-Hop Culture, and The Public Sphere.* Boston, MA: Northeastern UP, 2004. Print.

Pratt, Minnie Bruce. "Gender Quiz." *Available Means: An Anthology of Women's Rhetoric(s).* Ed. Joy Ritchie and Kate Ronald. Pittsburgh, PA: U of Pittsburgh P, 2001. 425–34. Print.

Rich, Adrienne. "When We Dead Awaken: Writing as Re-Vision." *Available Means: An Anthology of Women's Rhetoric(s).* Ed. Joy Ritchie and Kate Ronald. Pittsburgh, PA: U of Pittsburgh P, 2001. 268–81. Print.

Ritchie, Joy, and Kate Ronald, eds. *Available Means: An Anthology of Women's Rhetoric(s).* Pittsburgh, PA: U of Pittsburgh P, 2001. Print.

Royster, Jacqueline Jones. *Traces of a Stream: Literacy and Social Change Among African American Women.* Pittsburgh, PA: U of Pittsburgh P, 2000. Print.

Trinh, T. Minh-ha. *Woman, Native, Other: Writing, Postcoloniality, and Feminism.* Bloomington: Indiana UP, 1989. Print.

Walker, Alice. "In Search of Our Mothers' Gardens." *Available Means: An Anthology of Women's Rhetoric(s).* Ed. Joy Ritchie and Kate Ronald. Pittsburgh, PA: U of Pittsburgh P, 2001. 315–22. Print.

Woolf, Virginia. "Professions for Women." *Available Means: An Anthology of Women's Rhetoric(s).* Ed. Joy Ritchie and Kate Ronald. Pittsburgh, PA: U of Pittsburgh P, 2001. 242–46. Print.

For Further Reading

Foss, Karen A., Sonja K. Foss, and Cindy L. Griffin. *Feminist Rhetorical Theories.* Thousand Oaks, CA: Sage Publications, 1999. Print.

Lu, Min-Zhan. "From Silence to Words: Writing as Struggle." *Women/Writing/Teaching.* Ed. Jan Zlotnik Schmidt. Albany: SUNY P, 1998. 133–48. Print.

Scott, Jerrie Cobb, Dolores Y. Straker, and Laurie Katz, eds. *Affirming Students' Right to their Own Language: Bridging Language Policies and Pedagogical Practices.* New York: Routledge, 2008. Print.

Worsham, Lynn. "Writing Against Writing: The Predicament of *Ecriture Féminine* in Composition Studies." *Feminism and Composition: A Critical Sourcebook*. Ed. Gesa Kirsch et al. Boston, MA: Bedford/St. Martin's, 2003. 103–23. Print.

4 Teacher and Student Identity Through a Feminist Lens

Like feminist rhetoric, feminist scholarship on composition pedagogy illuminates subjectivity as an ever-present factor in how we teach writing, interact with students, and conceive of our goals as writers and teachers. For this reason, when I work with new teachers of writing, I encourage them to articulate how they imagine their roles or identities as teachers—and to then inquire into how that identity informs their relationship with students. One way to begin this articulation, I tell them, is to locate a metaphor for themselves as teachers.

My students have come up with a range of rich metaphors, from orchestral conductors, prompting students' individual contributions in concert with others; to gardeners, attending to local landscapes and sponsoring student growth; to jazz musicians, combining pedagogical improvisation with scholarly traditions and best practices. As these teachers gain experience, I notice that they come to see their roles not as singular or fixed but as ever adapting to their students' needs and interests. They come to see the act of teaching as similar to the act of rhetorically sensitive writing, requiring different strategies, approaches, and demeanors depending on the moment, the context, the purpose. As Amy Lee writes, "In our classrooms, most of us probably act as *bricoleurs*, deploying strategies associated with a variety of seemingly competing pedagogies depending on the situation at hand" (49). Implicit in Lee's quotation is the notion that particular strategies and teaching practices tend to be associated with specific pedagogical modes or schools of thought, but feminist scholars also illuminate how particular teacher and student *identities* are linked to different pedagogical approaches.

In this chapter, I trace key metaphors for the composition teacher, and subsequent roles for students, which emerge from several pedagogical movements. Even as these metaphors are associated with particular historical movements in the field, each of these remains alive today, functioning in both enabling and constraining ways. As I trace these metaphors, I highlight how feminist scholars have complicated these identities, shedding light on the gendered assumptions that shape them. Feminist contributions, in fact, have played a central role in establishing teachers' identities as multiple and changing, making room for contemporary teachers—like those in my class—to create their own metaphors for their roles in the classroom.

The Teacher as the (Feminized) Disciplinarian: Cleaning Student Texts, Cleaning Students

There is good reason that many people picture the writing teacher wielding a red pen and a scowl, ready to correct any misuse of grammar or punctuation that she confronts. Indeed, when I recently told another parent at my child's school that I teach composition, she said, "Oh, your daughter will never get away with anything!" The image of composition teacher as disciplinarian looms large in our cultural imagination.

If you think back to the Harvard origin story I described in Chapter 1, there is a clear connection between the writing teacher and the disciplinarian. As you'll recall, the course emerged when a test revealed that many incoming Harvard students were not fluent in their "mother tongue"; they could not speak and write, that is, according to Harvard standards. If you listen to the words of the exam readers, they understood the students to not only need linguistic remediation but character molding, as well. As one evaluator wrote, "It would certainly not seem unreasonable to insist that young men of nineteen years of age who present themselves for a college education should be able to [. . .] write their mother tongue with ease and correctness" (Adams et al., qtd. in Crowley 70). Another expressed dismay that "such a degree of immaturity should exist in a body of young men averaging nineteen years of age, coming from the best preparatory schools in America, and belonging to the most well-to-do and highly educated families" (Adams et al., qtd. in Crowley 70). Indeed, the subtext of these comments seems to ask: Who *raised* these young men?

Feminist composition scholar Susan Miller argues that the cultural image of the composition teacher—at Harvard and beyond—is akin to the nineteenth-century bourgeois mother and maid, which is an inherently contradictory role. On the one hand, the composition teacher is expected to serve as a maternal figure, displaying qualities "much like those of the mythologized mother: self-sacrifice, 'dedication,' 'caring,' and enormous capacities for untheorized attention to detail" ("Feminization" 526–27). On the other, the composition teacher occupies the role of the nineteenth-century maid, who often had disciplinary power over a child's education. In this way, she symbolized "authority, precision, and eternally validated, impeccable linguistic taste" (527). As Miller points out, these are the qualities that lead people who meet composition teachers to expect "censure and disapproval" (527).

The composition teacher's authority, however, is not a brand associated with external power. Just as a mother may have authority over her children, it is not an authority that translates readily into other sites. Similarly, while the composition instructor may wield authority over her students' language, historically, she is more likely to be a source of blame for students' poor writing than a resource for knowledge about how the university can improve student learning. As Miller writes, "The perduring image of the composition teacher is of a figure at once powerless and sharply authoritarian, occupying the transgressive, low-status site from which language may be arbitrated" (*Textual* 139).

In fact, because composition was considered a "low status" service site, the feminization of the composition teacher soon became literal as well as metaphorical, with first-year writing increasingly taught by women. This development was often assumed to reflect a "natural" match between task and subject—that is, that women were presumably "best suited" for this work. For instance, in her 1924 article "Academic Status of Women on University Faculties," Ella Lonn reported that English department chairs frequently indicated that "women do a better job of routine work, such as freshman composition, than men, as they are 'painstaking, conscientious, and enthusiastic'" (8). Further, "in positions of low salary, involving much drudgery," women were assumed to "do better than men, but solely because they are more nearly tied to the business of teaching than men" (8). Along similar lines, in 1930 Stith Thompson offered this comment in a survey of teaching conditions within freshman English: "[Women instructors] do often seem to be willing to settle down to a life of efficient freshman teaching without any idea of going further in their academic career" (qtd. in Connors 121).

While much has changed since the early twentieth century, the idea of the composition teacher as a feminized disciplinarian whose role is to prepare students for later, more important work has by no means disappeared. Take, for instance, this contemporary example: The widely-publicized 2011 critique of postsecondary education, *Academically Adrift: Limited Learning on College Campuses*, opens with a quotation from former Harvard president, Derek Bok, who complains that many students graduate college "without being able to write well enough to satisfy their employers" (Arum and Roksa 1). While the failure here is focused on workforce preparation rather than linguistic character, as in the Harvard origin story, composition teachers continue to feel external pressure to teach toward educational goals someone else has defined.

Feminist compositionists have challenged this metaphor of teacher as feminized disciplinarian by tracing its emergence in our field's history and heightening our attention to the "gendered, cultural call to identity" (Miller, "Feminization" 520) teachers continue to experience. That is, feminist scholars remind us to consider how identities emerge within a cultural context, so to disrupt these identities, we also need to challenge the culture that informs them. In today's climate, this means asking questions like these: Whose responsibility is it to teach writing? To what ends do we teach writing? How do our field's goals for writers and writing instruction connect and collide with the university's? With those expressed by employers or legislators? How is teacher knowledge considered in making these decisions? By disrupting the metaphor of the composition teacher as feminized disciplinarian serving externally-defined purposes, feminists in composition insist that writing teachers must play a central role in determining the aims and ends of writing instruction.

In the next section, I turn to another significant metaphor for the composition teacher—the composition teacher as nurturer.

For Writing and Discussion

1. One contributing factor to the literal feminization of composition teaching in the early twentieth century was the requirement of a PhD for professor positions. Women were less likely to complete their doctoral work—likely due to family demands and institutionalized sexism—and therefore filled the instruc-

tor ranks, where they could often work part-time. How do you imagine the identities of the teacher/instructor versus the professor were conceived? How do you see these categories as tied to gender constructions and assumptions? Do you still see evidence of these categories today?

2. Consider your experience as a student in or teacher of first-year composition. To what extent do you think the metaphor of composition teacher as disciplinarian endures today?

3. Recently several organizations in Composition Studies released a "Framework for Success in Postsecondary Writing," which focuses on habits of mind that make students successful college writers, including curiosity, openness, responsibility, flexibility, and metacognition or reflection. You can find this document at http://www.ncte.org/library/NCTEFiles/Resources/Positions/Framework%20one-pager_4-2011.pdf. How does this conception of students' needs—and therefore, how the role of teachers and students are understood—revise early correction-based models? Does this statement mesh with your own understanding of what college writers need? Why or why not?

The Composition Teacher as (Maternal) Nurturer

In her foundational 1988 article, "Composing as a Woman," Elizabeth A. Flynn observes that during the 1970s and 1980s, the field replaced the "figure of an authoritative father with an image of a nurturing mother" (423). While scholars like Miller, mentioned above, would insist that the "authoritative father" was actually a feminized subject, Flynn's point is that the role of the writing instructor shifted from a corrector of student prose to a sponsor of students' expression.

The revised understanding of the teacher coincided with a changed conception of the purpose and process of writing instruction. During the 1960s and 1970s, as writers like Hélène Cixous, Audre Lorde, and Adrienne Rich contributed to a growing body of feminist prose, composition established itself as a discipline with a subject worthy of study: the writing process. This resulted in a thread of scholarship that employed a scientific, cognitive approach to understanding students' composing processes—a movement I trace in the third origin story of Chapter 1. The "process movement" also produced a large body of work that dramatically changed the teaching of writing. Composition scholar Lad Tobin offers this caricature of the shift, which will give you a sense of how process pedagogy altered writing instruction and conceptions of students' and teachers' roles:

> Writing teachers, realizing, finally, that less is often more, began throwing things overboard—grammar lessons, lectures on usage, old chestnut assignments, the modes of discourse sequence, prose models, grades, rules, prescriptions. And they began experimenting with exciting new techniques—freewriting, mapping, peer editing groups, one-to-one conferences, writing workshops, portfolios. Students began to write essays that other humans might actually want to read. And, not coincidentally, teachers began to think that composition wasn't just a service course, a burden, a dues-paying debt on the way to real teaching, but actually a real field in its own right and, for some, even a calling. (4)

As you can see, this new conception of writing instruction required a different kind of teacher, one who plays a supporting, rather than leading, role in students' learning. Some teacher metaphors that emerged during the early process movement included midwife, facilitator, coach, and nurturer. As Donald M. Murray writes, "To be a teacher of a process [. . .] takes qualities too few of us have, but which most of us can develop. We have to be quiet, to listen, to respond. We are not the initiator or the motivator; we are the reader, the recipient" (5). In this context, then, the teacher's job is to create an atmosphere in which students can engage in the writing process and then to get out of the way, so that students can discover their own lines of inquiry.

Nowhere is this message more blatant than in Peter Elbow's best known book, *Writing Without Teachers*, which aims to help writers overcome constraints that prohibit their process—namely, those that place more emphasis on what is wrong than on what is possible. Freewriting is one foundational practice Elbow offers to aid writers in experiencing "uncensored" drafting; it involves putting pen to paper, or fingers to keys, without stopping. The idea is to write purely to discover, without questioning, doubting, or rejecting your own words. I use the term writer here, because in the class Elbow conceives, both student and teacher are writers; the teacher writes with the students, shows him or herself in process alongside the students. This, for Elbow, is part of what makes a "teacherless classroom," as does the requirement that a teacher acts "more the role of a learner and less the role of a teacher" (vii).

The process approach held much in common with feminist principles, and this moment was marked by what Joy Ritchie and Kathleen Boardman describe as an "intuitive connection" between composition and feminism. They write, the "emerging pedagogical theories [of the 1970s] spoke a language that resonated with feminism's concerns of the time: coming to voice and consciousness, illuminating experience and its relationship to individual identity, playing the believing game rather than the doubting game, collaborating rather than competing, subverting hierarchy in the classroom" (593). Even so, they note, there were limits to these connections and conceptions, which in some ways risked reinforcing the very conditions feminists sought to challenge.

For instance, some feminist scholars called attention to the problems with celebrating a "feminized" or maternal teacher identity. Susan C. Jarratt argues that because male and female teachers are not read as equally positioned authority figures, a male teacher's adoption of a supportive, nurturing role means something different than it does for a woman. Think, for instance, of the way a father pushing a stroller down the street is often praised for caring for his child, while a woman doing the same thing is simply understood to be fulfilling her "natural" role. Fixed assumptions about cultural identities limit the range of roles women are allowed to play in the classroom. As Jarratt observes, the assumption that a female teacher will be nurturing and supportive puts her "at a disadvantage in any attempt to assert a counterhegemonic authority as a woman" (268). Eileen E. Schell goes further to suggest that the image of the teacher as caring, sacrificing, and maternal is often held "in opposition to the stereotype of the 'arid, strident' feminist teacher" (553), representing a no-win dichotomy for the female teacher.

Feminist scholars also challenge the notion of a "teacherless" classroom, where all writers can coexist as equals. To assume such an atmosphere exists, they argue, is to overlook the real power dynamics that exist both between teacher and student and among students, themselves. Jarratt, for instance, argues that differences among subjects pervade the writing classrooms in which we teach and learn, and "such inequities often make the attempt to create a harmonious and nurturing community of readers an illusory fiction—a superficial suturing of real social divisions" (267).

Even with these problems, process pedagogy's revision of student and teacher identity allowed the field to break away from correction-based models of writing and made room for personal experience in an academy that often discredited its value. However, feminist scholars remind us that it is not enough to simply value the "feminine" teacher or "nurturing" environment without examining the social structures and values that contribute to dichotomies like feminine/masculine, nurturing/authoritative, affective/intellectual in the first place. The next pedagogical movement—the social turn—begins to engage the concerns raised by Schell and Jarratt, attending to the roles of teachers and students as contingent upon cultural context, power dynamics, and multiple aspects of social location.

For Writing and Discussion

1. Can you think of examples in your own learning where you've experienced elements of the process pedagogies described above—that is, where teachers might have incorporated practices like freewriting, peer response, and writing-to-learn projects and/or where teachers actively sought to disrupt traditional power dynamics in the classroom? What were the limits and possibilities of these moments for you as a learner?

2. Have you had experiences where teachers seemed to challenge (implicitly or explicitly) assumptions about gender roles in the classroom? To what extent are women allowed to adopt traditionally "male" and "female" traits in their identities as teachers?

Writing Teacher, Critical Teacher

In her book *Composing Critical Pedagogies: Teaching Writing as Revision*, Lee illustrates a classroom moment where she invites students to generate a list of all the terms they can think of for several different categories of people: male, female, heterosexual, homosexual, white person, and black person. She then asks them to indicate whether the terms evoke either immediately negative or positive connotations (marked with a – or +). Here is what the students list for male and female:

> **male**: guy, man+, dude, boy, stud+, prick–
>
> **female**: chick–, woman, girl (sometimes–), babe–, broad–, bitch–, cunt–, skirt–, piece of ass– (42).

As the conversation ensues, Lee's students come to see that while we can easily point to negative terms for women and people of color, it is difficult to locate a term for a white man that has the same level of negative connotations. They also note that not all terms mean the same things in all contexts. Female friends may affectionately call each other "chicks," but they may find it offensive when men use the term. As Lee writes, "The signification of the naming is largely context-bound, embedded in the relationship between who is speaking to whom and why" (43).

Here Lee is a significantly different kind of teacher than the corrector or the nurturer. Different, too, is the role of students, who are not only writers but are also investigators of the social nature of language—asking how it works and examining its consequences. This classroom focus emerged during the 1980s, when composition took a "social turn" to emphasize the role that language, writing, and rhetoric play in shaping how we understand ourselves and the world around us. Just as feminist thinkers like T. Minh-ha Trinh and Gloria Anzaldúa articulated the connection between language, culture, and identity, composition shifted its conception of writing from a neutral vehicle for transmitting already-determined knowledge or for expressing individual identity to the means through which we construct—and can change—reality.

During this moment, Composition Studies was greatly influenced by an educational movement called critical pedagogy. Paulo Freire, a Brazilian educator, is considered a founder of this movement. Through literacy instruction, Freire sought to empower peasants to become aware of the social structures that oppressed them and to alter those structures through action and reflection, or praxis. He is perhaps best known for challenging the "banking model" of education, where students are constructed as passive receptacles into whom teachers deposit knowledge. Instead, he offers a vision of liberatory, or critical, education, in which learners engage in dialogue with teachers to challenge existing social dynamics, not simply adapt to them.

Freire's work propelled educators to transport his vision of liberatory pedagogy to US students. This body of work, critical pedagogy, is often credited to a few male theorists with roots in the discipline of education—Henry Giroux, Peter McLaren, and Ira Shor. Ira Shor's 1980 *Critical Teaching and Everyday Life* offers an early illustration of these theories in practice (19). Built upon Freire's notion of problem-posing education, Shor articulates a pedagogy that teaches students to examine how their lives, which are shaped by consumer-culture and media icons, can seem inevitable and unchangeable. He dubs this "pre-scientific thinking," which rests on belief in luck, chance, and common sense (66). The critical teacher helps students to "extraordinarily reexperience the ordinary" (93), that is, to see, through a critical lens, how cultural norms and practices shape their lives.

Mass media and popular culture became a common focus for the critical classroom, allowing students to examine how dominant culture—in the form of advertisements, TV shows, film, websites—is constructed through language in ways that perpetuate consumerism and inequity. Using writing to critically analyze the world around them, students are positioned as cultural participants who can challenge and reconstruct their own realities—even as they cannot entirely escape the way culture writes them.

The role of the teacher during the social turn, then, becomes one of problem-poser (Freire) who prompts students to question assumptions, normative readings, familiar stories. David Bartholomae, a composition scholar associated with this school of thought, offers an example of this role. He describes a student who writes an essay about her parents' divorce. "We've all read this essay," he writes. "We've read it because the student cannot invent a way of talking about family, sex roles, separation. Her essay is determined by a variety of forces: the genre of the personal essay as it has shaped this student and this moment; attitudes about the family and divorce; the figures of 'Father' and 'Mother' and 'Child' and so on" (484). We could, he acknowledges, aid the student's writing process by "letting her believe [the essay] is hers" (484)—that is, as a unique expression of herself, within her control. The teacher, in this case, might ask for more details or attend to the piece's voice. Instead, he wants the student to see that the story is already written by culture. As he writes, "I ask her to revise in such a way that the order of the essay is broken—to write against the grain of the discourse that has determined her account of her family. I begin by being dismissive" (502). Here the teacher's job is to prompt the student to unravel and critique, rather than reproduce, a "predictable version of the family" (502).

While the practice of challenging restrictive cultural norms is one feminist scholars share with critical pedagogies, feminists have played a key role in disrupting some of the depictions of the teacher (and students) promoted within critical pedagogy discourse. In particular, feminists have challenged the idea of the teacher as what Giroux calls a "bearer of critical knowledge" (90), who has critical knowledge the students presumably lack. For instance, in teaching a course on media and anti-racism, Elizabeth Ellsworth notes that as a white, middle-class professor, she cannot claim to understand racism better than her students, "especially those students of color coming into class after six months (or more) of campus activism and whole lives of experience and struggle against racism" (99). Ellsworth further critiques the construction of an "enlightened" teacher, who presumably exists outside of the cultural dynamics she analyzes and critiques. She writes, "No teacher is free of these learned and internalized oppressions. Nor are accounts of one group's suffering and struggle immune from reproducing narratives oppressive to another's—the racism of the women's movement in the United States is one example" (99).

Similarly, a feminist reading might challenge Bartholomae's example of the student's narrative on her parents' divorce. What does it mean to begin by "being dismissive"? To assume that the teacher has a better or more critical way of understanding that moment? To position the students as in need of "critical knowledge," and the teacher as the one who can provide it, feminist scholars argue, risks reproducing a hierarchical dynamic and relationship that critical teaching aims to disrupt. Patricia Bizzell further notes that the privileging of an "academic worldview" that values skepticism, critique, debate, and "objectivity" may devalue the knowledge students bring to class and limit possibilities for new forms of intellectual work (2, 5).

Feminist scholars also complicate the notion that the role of "critical teacher" is equally available to all subjects. Lil Brannon argues that the image of the critical teacher is built on a narrative of masculine heroism—think Robin Williams in *Dead Poet's Society*—who can create a student-centered classroom and at the same time, maintain unquestioned authority and intellect. She observes that when critical educators argue that the teacher should know when to "wither away" and hand authority over to students, they overlook the historical circumstances of female teachers, who have historically been denied authority; to wither away risks reinforcing the invisibility of female authority. Feminist pedagogues, alternatively, encourage teachers to pay close attention to how power dynamics function in local classrooms with the particular students we teach, arguing that sweeping theoretical prescriptions can limit as much as enable critical goals.

Social turn or critical pedagogies opened new purposes and possibilities for the writing classroom, and new roles for writing teachers and students to use language to do cultural work—to critique and rewrite their realities. However, feminist scholars insist that this work must involve reflexivity and humility, so that the teachers' agenda and knowledge does not overwrite that of the students. This brings us to the current moment when feminist compositionists articulate the role of the teacher as reflexive, rhetorically sensitive, multiple, and dynamic.

For Writing and Discussion

1. One ongoing debate around social constructivist and critical pedagogies deals with the extent to which "politics" belong in the classroom. Those opposed to critical pedagogies fear that students will be indoctrinated by the teacher's political agenda. Critical teachers argue that all pedagogies are political; they all promote some kind of ideology and shape students' understanding of the world. Where do you stand on this question? Why?

2. While social constructivist pedagogies are often seen as a critique of expressivist-process approaches, where do you see commonalities among them? What possibilities might exist by bringing the two together? Are there elements that cannot, finally, be reconciled?

3. What connections do you see between the emphasis on the local that feminist pedagogies call for here and the attention devoted to personal experience as knowledge addressed in earlier chapters?

Where We Are, Where We're Headed: The Composition Teacher as Rhetor

As composition moves into the twenty-first century, we see pedagogical approaches that move from predetermined roles for teachers and students to instead promote multiplicity and rhetorical sensitivity. Contemporary writing pedagogies commonly meld approaches earned from the field's history of inquiry and practice—social constructivist notions of language, rhetorical awareness, writing as a process—with new attention to diverse forms; multiple, shifting student and teacher subjectivities; and ever-changing technologies.

In today's classrooms, students are often asked to contribute to conversations that matter to them by making deliberate decisions about form, language, and audience. Composition textbooks include multiple forms ranging from blogs to essays to paintings to comics, emphasizing the myriad ways writing animates our culture. While academic discourse remains the focus in some composition programs, others focus on rhetoric, public discourse, personal narrative, and digital literacies.

As forms and purposes of composing multiply, so does the notion of diversity and identity in the classroom—and feminist scholars have led the way in these conversations. In the last fifteen years alone, as we have seen feminist rhetoric expand and diversify, we also see increased representation of the vast range of students and teachers who occupy composition classrooms. Harriet Malinowitz's *Textual Orientations: Lesbian and Gay Students and the Making of Discourse Communities* helps us to understand the connections among sexuality, writing, and authority and extends our conception of gender in the writing classroom (xviii). Scholars like Donna LeCourt and Mary Soliday remind us that social class needs to be considered alongside ethnicity, race, and gender as we consider the experience of our students. Jennifer Seibel Trainor and Amy E. Winans (among others) illuminate whiteness as an oft-invisible racial identity essential to include within discussions of race and social inequity.

Just as the attention to students' social locations becomes more complex, so too does that of the teacher. One key difference between the critical pedagogy described above and the feminist-critical pedagogies that follow is with how the teacher's location and role is theorized. Rather than presumed to act out of a single identity (authority, liberator, woman, lesbian, working-class member, etc.), the teacher is necessarily multiply situated. For instance, even as they highlight working-class performances in their 2011 article "Teachers with(out) Class: Transgressing Academic Social Space through Working-Class Performances," Donna LeCourt and Anna Rita Napoleone emphasize that "working-class subjectivities are always intersectional subjectivities, made different through the transecting axes of race, ethnicity, region, age, sexuality, and gender" (103). Likewise, Michelle Gibson, Martha Marinara, and Deborah Meem call attention to the interconnections of class, gender, and sexuality in their article "Bi, Butch, and Bar Dyke: Pedagogical Performances of Class, Gender, and Sexuality" and illuminate the "differences within difference" inside of all social categories (471).

Feminist scholars also disrupt fixed expectations about how the feminist or critical teacher must behave. Instead, many argue for a rhetorical approach to the pedagogies teachers perform, which is based on the local context, exigency, power dynamics, and subjects involved. Julie Jung puts it this way:

> The knowledge that pedagogical performance is a rhetorical choice rather than the 'natural' consequence of identity (Feminist Teacher) challenges universalist claims about how feminists and other oppositional teachers "should" teach. Rather than begin with claims to identity, a strategy that repeatedly offered me nothing but binary options, I can instead foreground my feminist-motivated pedagogical purpose [. . .] With this goal in mind, I can redefine teaching "styles"—i.e. nurturing, traditional, and confrontational—as performance genres and generate disruption by self-consciously juxtaposing them within the classroom space. (147)

Of course, this does not mean that the teacher is in full control of her performance, or that she can finally control how students read her. As LeCourt and Napoleone contend, "How [our] performances are read [. . .] depends much upon the particularities of the academic social spaces in which we are located and the power differentials among the actors in those spaces" (87).

This approach does, however, disrupt ideas that there is a "right" way to enact a feminist classroom to instead emphasize the importance of kairos—a term from classical rhetoric meaning the opportune occasion for speech. Attending to kairos means taking into account rhetorical circumstances and contingencies including audience, social dynamics, message, and timing to choose the most effective way to communicate. Karen Kopelson, for instance, writes about the ambiguity she experiences over whether to come out to her students as lesbian. Finally, she concludes, "I'm afraid I cannot offer one-size-fits-all advice for what all gay/lesbian teachers should do, for how they should "be queer" in the classroom, or for how queer they should be" (569). She goes on to write that coming out (or not) is an intensely personal choice, but it is also "a rhetorical act, one dependent on context, intention, and audience reception" (569).

Increasingly, then, we begin to see a more reciprocal dynamic between composition instruction and rhetorical theory, with feminists employing rhetorical strategies to create new possibilities for their students' texts and for the conception of teachers' and students' roles. This contemporary work was made possible, however, only because of the important feminist contributions that preceded it—work that established identity and experience as deserving of inquiry and attention. In the next chapter, I focus on how feminist compositionists established subjectivity as an important resource for knowledge in both the writing classroom and composition research.

For Writing and Discussion

1. How do our conceptions of "self"—how we understand the nature of identity—change over the time period traced in this chapter?

2. This chapter follows ideas of students and teachers, language, and pedagogies across three key movements in the field: current-traditionalism, process/expressivism, and social constructivist/critical pedagogy. Where do you see the greatest shifts in these understandings over time? Where do you see remnants of "the old" in articulations of "the new"?

Works Cited

Arum, Richard, and Josipa Roksa. *Academically Adrift: Limited Learning on College Campuses*. Chicago, IL: U of Chicago P, 2011. Print.

Bartholomae, David. "Writing with Teachers: A Conversation with Peter Elbow." *Cross-Talk in Comp Theory*. Ed. Victor Villanueva, Jr. Urbana, IL: NCTE, 1997. 479–509. Print.

Bizzell, Patricia. "The Intellectual Work of 'Mixed' Forms of Academic Discourses." *Alt Dis: Alternative Discourses in the Academy*. Ed. Christopher Schroeder, Helen Fox, and Patricia Bizzell. Portsmouth, NH: Boynton/Cook, Heinemann, 2002. 1–10. Print.

Brannon, Lil. "M[other]: Lives on the Outside." *Written Communication* 10.3 (1993): 457–65. Print.

Connors, Robert J. "Overwork/Underpay: Labor and Status of Composition Teachers Since 1880." *Rhetoric Review* 9.1 (1990): 108–26). Print.

Crowley, Sharon. *Composition in the University: Historical and Polemical Essays*. Pittsburgh, PA: U of Pittsburgh P, 1998. Print.

Elbow, Peter. *Writing without Teachers*. New York: Oxford UP, 1998. Print.

Ellsworth, Elizabeth. "Why Doesn't this Feel Empowering? Working Through the Repressive Myths of Critical Pedagogy." *Feminisms and Critical Pedagogy*. Ed. Carmen Luke and Jennifer Gore. New York: Routledge, 1992. 90–119. Print.

Flynn, Elizabeth A. "Composing as a Woman." *College Composition and Communication* 39 (1988): 423–35. Print.

Freire, Paulo. *Pedagogy of the Oppressed*. New York: Continuum Publishing, 2000. Print.

Gibson, Michelle, Martha Marinara, and Debora Meem. "Bi, Butch, and Bar Dyke: Pedagogical Performances of Class, Gender, and Sexuality." *Feminism and Composition: A Critical Sourcebook*. Ed. Gesa Kirsch et al. Boston, MA: Bedford/St. Martin's, 2003. 466–87. Print.

Giroux, Henry. *Schooling and the Struggle for Public Life: Critical Pedagogy in the Modern Age*. Minneapolis, University of MN Press, 1988. Print.

Jarratt, Susan C. "Feminism and Composition: A Case for Conflict." *Feminism and Composition: A Critical Sourcebook*. Ed. Gesa Kirsch et al. Boston, MA: Bedford/St. Martin's, 2003. 263–80. Print.

Jung, Julie. *Revisionary Rhetoric, Feminist Pedagogy, and Multigenre Texts*. Carbondale: Southern Illinois UP, 2005. Print.

Kopelson, Karen. "Of Ambiguity and Erasure: The Perils of Performative Pedagogy." *Relations, Locations, Positions: Composition Theory for Writing Teachers*. Ed. Peter Vandenberg, Sue Hum, and Jennifer Clary-Lemon. Urbana, IL: NCTE, 2006. 563–70. Print.

LeCourt, Donna, and Anna Rita Napoleone. "Teachers with(out) Class: Transgressing Academic Social Space through Working-Class Performances." *Pedagogy* 11.1 (2011): 81–108. Print.

Lee, Amy. *Composing Critical Pedagogies: Teaching Writing as Revision.* Urbana, IL: NCTE, 2000. Print.

Lonn, Ella. "Academic Status of Women on University Faculties." *Journal of the American Association of University Women* 17 (1924): 5–11. Print.

Malinowitz, Harriet. *Textual Orientations: Lesbian and Gay Students and the Making of Discourse Communities.* Portsmouth, NH: Boynton/Cook, 1995. Print.

Miller, Susan. "The Feminization of Composition." *Feminism and Composition: A Critical Sourcebook.* Ed. Gesa Kirsch et al. Boston, MA: Bedford/St. Martin's, 2003. 520–33. Print.

—. *Textual Carnivals: The Politics of Composition.* Carbondale: Southern Illinois UP, 1993. Print.

Murray, Donald M. "Teach Writing as a Process Not Product." *Cross-Talk in Composition Theory.* Ed. Victor Villanueva, Jr. Urbana, IL: NCTE, 1997. 1–6. Print.

Ritchie, Joy, and Kathleen Boardman. "Feminism in Composition: Inclusion, Metonymy, and Disruption." *College Composition and Communication* 50 (1999): 585–606. Print.

Schell, Eileen E. "The Feminization of Composition: Questioning the Metaphors That Bind Women Teachers." *Feminism and Composition: A Critical Sourcebook.* Ed. Gesa Kirsch et al. Boston, MA: Bedford/St. Martin's, 2003. 552–57. Print.

Shor, Ira. *Critical Teaching and Everyday Life.* Chicago, IL: U of Chicago P, 1987. Print.

Soliday, Mary. "Class Dismissed." *College English* 61 (1999): 731–41. Print.

Tobin, Lad. "How the Writing Process Was Born—and Other Conversion Narratives." *Taking Stock: The Writing Process Movement in the '90s.* Ed. Lad Tobin and Thomas Newkirk. Portsmouth, NH: Boynton/Cook, 1994. 1–14. Print.

Trainor, Jennifer Seibel. "Critical Pedagogy's 'Other': Constructions of Whiteness in Education for Social Change." *College Composition and Communication* 53 (2002): 631–50. Print.

Winans, Amy E. "Local Pedagogies and Race: Interrogating White Safety in the Rural College Classroom." *College English* 67 (2005): 253–73. Print.

For Further Reading

Herrington, Anne, and Marcia Smith Curtis. *Persons in Process: Four Stories of Writing and Development in College.* Urbana, IL: NCTE, 2000. Print.

Luke, Carmen, and Jennifer Gore, eds. *Feminisms and Critical Pedagogy.* New York: Routledge, 1992. Print.

Payne, Michelle. "Rend(er)ing Women's Authority in the Writing Classroom." *Taking Stock: The Writing Process Movement in the '90s.* Ed. Lad Tobin and Thomas Newkirk. Portsmouth, NH: Boynton/Cook, 1994. 97–114. Print.

Qualley, Donna. *Turns of Thought: Teaching Composition as Reflexive Inquiry.* Portsmouth, NH: Boynton/Cook, 1997. Print.

Yee, Marian. "Are You the Teacher?" *Composition and Resistance.* Ed. Mark C. Hurlbert and Michael Blitz. Portsmouth, NH: Boynton/Cook, 1991. 24–30. Print.

5 Research and Writing Through a Feminist Lens: A Focus on Experience

Early in my first-year composition course, I ask my students to generate a list of rules they have learned throughout their educational lives about what constitutes "good writing." I write on the board as they call out ideas.

"It needs to flow," one student says.

"What does that mean?" I ask. "What is 'flow' in writing?"

"Good transitions," another student interjects. "One paragraph needs to logically lead to the next."

I add that to the board as a student calls out, "There needs to be a thesis statement in the first, or maybe second, paragraph, so the reader knows what the paper is about."

"You can't use contractions," another student adds.

"Never?" I ask.

"Well," she reconsiders, "not in a formal paper, like a research paper."

"And in a research paper," her classmate explains, "you can't use your own opinion. Or at least you can't make it look like it's your own opinion."

"Yeah, like you can't use 'I'," another student clarifies. "Research is supposed to be objective."

I invite my students to generate this list so we can look again at rules about writing that we have come to take for granted. Instead of approaching these rules as neutral and universal, we consider the assumptions and values that shape them. As you may notice in the students' final comments, one of the most powerful assumptions about academic or scholarly writing is that it is "objective." Indeed, this notion harks back to the third origin story I describe in Chapter 1, which privileges a scientific research model based on objective, quantifiable knowledge; it further resonates with privileged discourse within Classical Rhetoric. At the center of this model is an idealized academic persona, which tends to be (seemingly) objective, skeptical, argumentative, and logical. Consequently, I ask my students, what kinds of writing and writers does this ideal include and exclude? In addition to highlighting that our ideas of "good writing" are socially constructed in ways that tend to reflect the values and knowledge practices of privileged groups, I also invite students to consider how these rules and expectations have shaped their experiences as writers. How does leaving your "self" out of writing affect your experience of researching and composing? What would it mean to write from, and make visible, your interests and commitments? To include your experience as a resource of knowledge?

The issue of who is included and excluded by discursive norms is a central concerns for feminist scholars in Composition Studies. Since the 1970s, feminist compositionists have helped the field to see how discursive practices are shaped by gender in ways that impede women's experience of reading, writing, and learning. They sought to better understand women's experience of composing so as to discover the most effective ways to facilitate women's contributions as writers and thinkers. They also challenged normative practices of scholarly work, offering models that claimed, rather than transcended, the subjectivity of the writer and researcher. In what follows, I provide a closer look at this work.

Raising Consciousness of and about Women Writers

During the late 1960s and 1970s, the women's movement advocated for political change on behalf of women, and it also illuminated the connection between the political and the personal—making women's experiences an important site of investigation. Consciousness-raising groups, for instance, brought women together to discuss topics relevant to women's lives, from birth control to work discrimination to motherhood, in a safe setting that allowed women to make public what society often deemed private. Perhaps most importantly, these groups helped women to reexamine their lived experiences in light of wider social and political realities; that is, they highlighted how women's experiences were not simply "natural" or individual "problems" but were instead shaped by cultural expectations and definitions.

We can also see similar principles at play in early feminist composition scholarship. For instance, Florence Howe's 1971 essay "Identity and Expression: A Writing Course for Women," published in a special issue of *College English*, aims to help women students understand and challenge the social factors that have convinced them they are "inferior writers." Howe begins with the following observation:

> My women students consistently consider women writers (and hence themselves, though that is not said outright) inferior to men. If women believe themselves inferior writers, so it will be. [. . .] How to convince young women that their self-images grow not from their biology but from centuries of belief in their inferiority, as well as from the male-dominated and controlled institutions? (33)

She proposes a pedagogy, then, that invites women to articulate their experiences as writers and then to locate these experiences within "processes of social conditioning" (35). A form of consciousness-raising, Howe wants her students to examine their individual experiences in the context of cultural expectations and assumptions about female writers. Also central to this pedagogy is a classroom that feels safe and hospitable, so that women can write without feeling inferior or overly dependent on external validation (a grade, teacher approval, etc.)—think here of Woolf's "Angel in the House" described in Chapter 3—and have room to "grow conscious of themselves as women" (35). To this end, Howe relies on pedagogical practices that challenge academic norms. For instance, students determine their own deadlines, writing topics, and the form in which they compose. They also write daily, in order to prompt experimentation and exploration of ideas, and to participate in open-ended discussion. In addition to its ties to the feminist movement outside of the university, Howe's pedagogy also works in conversation with the expressivist-process movement within Composition Studies (described in the prior chapter)—which valued writing as a means of expression and self-discovery—and with the pedagogies employed by Women's Studies, both emerging in universities at the time.

Chapter 5: Research and Writing Through a Feminist Lens   73

By the mid-1980s, when women increasingly occupied tenure-track lines in the field and thus had more time to research, issues of how to sponsor women's learning were spotlighted. Pamela J. Annas's 1985 "Style as Politics: A Feminist Approach to the Teaching of Writing" is a notable example. Annas's piece shares Howe's project of making visible and challenging the social situation of female writers. Like Howe, Annas points to the difficulty women students—like so many of the women rhetors mentioned in the previous chapters—experience in "trying to find an authentic and effective writing voice [. . .] in the context of approved models of writing" (61). Consequently, she challenges the privileging of linear, impersonal, abstract writing over "sensual, contextual, and committed" writing, arguing that it is necessary for students to "discover their own voices in an expression, assertion, and grounding of their own identity in their own experience" (61). Importantly, Annas insists that the field should not distinguish "experiential" writing from the seemingly "rigorous" essay or research paper; instead, she argues for teaching writing that is "rigorous without sacrificing subjectivity" (62). In other words, she imagines a new mode of academic writing which, unlike the privileged notion of scientific objectivism, views subjectivity as a resource for, not a hindrance to, knowledge.

Annas recognizes, however, that establishing new discursive forms means working within and against existing expectations for writing. To this end, Annas and her students study the textual strategies employed by a range of female essayists (or, we might say, rhetors), such as Virginia Woolf, Adrienne Rich, and Gloria Anzaldúa, to consider how they negotiate composing in an "authentic female voice" in contexts that do not often value women's voices. As Annas explains, "Whenever a woman sits down to write, she is engaged in a complex political act in which the self and the world struggle in and through the medium of language" (63).

In order to facilitate her female students' writing processes, Annas asks them to compile a list of their own "writing blocks" and what underlies them (67). She then helps them to become aware of their own writing processes, so as to both demystify the writing process and to facilitate students' agency as writers. In discussing these topics with her students, Annas describes two primary writing problems: Some students are fluent in polished, correct prose but take few risks and tend to write in a "detached" and "passionless" style; others are comfortable writing informal prose but have difficulty making their writing public or accepting criticism that will enable the writing to reach an audience (69–70). She describes the tensions this way: "As women writers we have walked a fine line between objectivity and subjectivity, between self-censorship and self-indulgence, silence and noise, rigid control and little or no control" (70). Annas seeks, then, to help both groups of students move out of their comfort zones to establish a better balance between these two modes. Ultimately, she wants their writing—no matter the form—to merge the personal and the public and to stem from their own experiences and commitments:

> The kind of writing I finally want these students to be able to do brings together the personal and the political, the private and the public, into writing which is committed and powerful because it takes risks, because it speaks up clearly in their own voices and from their experience, experiments with techniques of argumentation and skillful organization, and engages, where appropriate, with the insights of other writers. (71)

In this way, then, feminist teachers helped women students to work both within and against discursive expectations—particularly those that taught them to sever themselves from their intellectual work.

For Writing and Discussion

1. Think of a time in your history as a student when you gained an understanding of a life experience or situation you may have taken for granted as, in fact, tied to social and cultural factors. What were the circumstances of that realization? What kind of learning did it facilitate?

2. In what ways do you see evidence that academic writing has become more open to different kinds of "academic personas"? In what ways do you see resistance to this change?

From Research on Gender to Feminist Research

One of the most cited indications of the union between Composition Studies and feminism is Elizabeth A. Flynn's 1988 article "Composing as a Woman."

Here Flynn makes the important observation that "the fields of feminist studies and composition studies have not engaged each other in a serious or systematic way," and calls for attention to the following questions: "Do males and females compose differently? Do they acquire language in different ways? Do research methods and research samples in composition reflect a male bias?" (245). Flynn proceeds to draw from foundational work in feminist studies—Nancy Chodorow's *The Reproduction of Mothering: Psychoanalysis and the Sociology of Gender*, Carol Gilligan's *In a Different Voice: Psychological Theory and Women's Development*, and Mary Field Belenky, Blyth Clinchy, Nancy Goldberger, and Jill Tarule's *Women's Ways of Knowing: The Development of Self, Voice, and Mind*—to examine how feminist insights about gender differences in social and psychological development influence women's writing. Her concern is that if male and female "writing strategies and patterns of representation do differ"—as she finds in her teaching experience and research—"then ignoring those differences almost certainly means a suppression of women's separate ways of thinking and writing" (251). Ultimately, Flynn's article served as an important call to the field to attend to gender—and to women's experiences—both in the classroom and in scholarship.

By 1992 a traceable line of feminist research in Composition Studies was established, which Patricia A. Sullivan documents in her essay "Feminism and Methodology in Composition Studies." She highlights the following as key feminist concerns within composition: 1) How does the gendered institution affect research and teaching practices? 2) How do gendered assumptions about writing inform the writing process and products we teach? 3) How do women learn, organize, and express knowledge, and make meaning from their particular cultural locations? (126). Feminist research practices, then, seek to illuminate and challenge masculinist structures and practices and to revise them in a way that makes room for alternative ways of knowing and being in the academy.

Sullivan argues, however, that the field has not moved far enough from studies that focus on *gender* to *feminist* studies. While the former aims to examine differences between genders, the latter seeks to overturn patriarchal assumptions and practices that "render women's experiences invisible and undervalued" (132). To further explain feminist research, Sullivan draws from the definition articulated by Sandra Harding, an influential feminist scientist: feminist research "generates its problematics from the perspective of women's experiences"; it is "designed for women" so as to "provide women explanations of social phenomena that they want and need; and it "insists that the inquirer her/himself be placed in the same critical plane as the overt subject matter" (Harding, qtd. in Sullivan 133). Here you'll notice that Harding rewrites the scientist from (seemingly) objective and distanced to necessarily subjective and committed. While the end goal of this research is not to replace a male-centered perspective with a female-centered one, Harding contends that it is necessary to focus singly on women's experience to highlight how assumptions of what is "natural" or "normal" are often gendered in a way that privileges males.

Although the field continues to draw upon and extend Harding's conception of feminist research, some of the most visible inroads in feminist composition scholarship focus on the relationship between inquirer and subject. As Sullivan notes, feminist research rejects the very idea of objective research methodologies; rather, all research is "interested" and affected not only by the researcher's perspective but also by cultural and institutional values, norms, and expectations. She writes, "The researcher's own race, class, culture, and gender assumptions are not neutral positions from which he or she observes the world but lenses that determine how and what the researcher sees" (136–37).

Feminist research in Composition Studies, then, increasingly relied on methodologies that made visible the lens of the researcher. These included practices like open-ended interviews and case studies, which enabled "researchers to generate descriptions of composing from the point of view and in the language of the writers they [were] studying;" participant observation, which allowed investigators to reflect on their own subjectivity as both researchers as writers; and teacher researchers, where teachers examined their own experience and the dynamics that shaped it, within the local site of the classroom (137). This is not to say that feminists rejected more traditional forms of research entirely, but that they sought to fuse their research with the values and goals of feminist theory and practice. Or as Sullivan puts it, "whether individual researchers are appropriating or revising conventions of empirical scholarship, their work is informed by the same purpose: They are consciously seeking to create the conditions and circumstances whereby voices, stories, and discourses too long silent in the academy can be heard" (137).

The growing presence of feminist scholarship in the field, however, did not guarantee its wide reception. Often, feminist work appeared in collections designated as "special issues" and was therefore bracketed off from the field's central conversations. Sullivan describes the situation this way:

> [Feminist] research is published in regular issues of our principal journals only when editors narrow their perceptions of audience exclusively to women or to feminist women and men. Research by and for men requires no such narrowing because the universal audience of composition scholarship, figured in the generic everyman, is already male. (135)

The ongoing challenge facing feminist scholarship, then, was to demonstrate its importance to the field at large—to show how attention to different voices, research strategies, and knowledges would benefit the field as a whole.

FOR WRITING AND DISCUSSION

1. What do you see as the limits and possibilities of arguing that women had a distinct way of experiencing writing and the writing process? Why might this argument have been historically necessary?

2. Locate a piece of research explicitly categorized as feminist. (A few feminist journals include *Differences: A Journal of Feminist Cultural Studies*, *Hypatia: A Journal of Feminist Philosophy*, *Journal of Women's History*, *Women and Health: A Multidisciplinary Journal of Women's Health Issues*, and *Signs: Journal of Women, Culture and Society*). How does the writer define feminist research? In what ways does it challenge research norms? In ways does it work within them?

The Evolving use of Experience

In the 2003 collection *Feminism and Composition, A Critical Sourcebook*, Flynn offers a reflective essay entitled "Contextualizing 'Composing as a Woman'," which considers what has changed since the publication of her 1988 piece—now heavily anthologized—and why historical context matters. As I soon discuss, Flynn's piece, as well as other early feminist work, would later be critiqued for relying too heavily on a dichotomous distinction between male and female writers and for overlooking difference within the category of women. However, as Flynn notes, context is crucial: She wrote the essay in a time when feminism was still not adequately present in the field of composition, a time when a strong stance was necessary. As she writes, "It was important, in the late 1980s, to make a powerful case for differences between men and women, even if we would later need to qualify, refine, and even contradict those claims" (341).

Indeed, much of the feminist scholarship that followed served to extend this early advocacy for women's experience by adding additional lenses through which to view both gender and experience. One important revision was a move away from perceptions of gender as a single, uniform identity category to one that is multiple and fluid and functions always in relationship with other subject positions. This means that gender must be examined alongside other social categories, including race, class, sexual orientation, family history, embodiment, etc.—some of which may marginalize while others may privilege; you can see examples of this in the work of Trinh T. Minh-ha, Min-Zhan Lu, and Minnie Bruce Pratt, mentioned in the previous chapter. As Joy S. Ritchie notes in her 1990 piece "Confronting the 'Essential' Problem: Reconnecting Feminist Theory and Pedagogy," "The strength of feminism is its ability to hold in tension an array of theoretical and practical perspectives and, thus, to arrive at a clearer understanding of the varied nature of women's positions" (85).

Because these multiple and sometimes contradictory identities affect women's experiences as researchers, writers, and teachers, feminist scholars called for increasing self-reflexivity about these positions. For instance, Ritchie and Gesa E. Kirsch draw upon Adrienne Rich's notion of "politics of location"—an acknowledgment of the effects of our multiple positions on ourselves and others—to argue that feminist researchers and teachers "must claim the legitimacy of our experience," but that claim must be "accompanied by a rigorously reflexive examining of ourselves as researches that is as careful as our observation of the object of our inquiry" (142). This call prompted questions like: What does it mean for a white, female academic to study a population of African-American, female literacy learners? Or for a white, middle-class, female teacher to lead a writing workshop in a male prison? Or for a young, lesbian teaching assistant to come out in her first-year composition classroom? Feminist scholars, then, asked not only "How are we marginalized as women?" but also "How do we marginalize, based on a Western perspective, white privilege, or class difference?" In this way, they approached power differently, viewing it not as something one gender or the other "holds" but rather as dynamic and fluid, informed by particular contexts, social locations, and histories—some explicit and knowable and some not.

We can see an example of rigorous self-reflexivity articulated in Jacqueline Jones Royster's study *Traces of a Stream: Literacy and Social Change Among African American Women*, which documents nineteenth-century African American women's rhetorical activism. In so doing, she considers (and complicates) her relationship and identification with the subjects she studies:

> There is constancy in the need for negotiation, beginning with the question of how much I actually do share identities with the women I study and how much I do not. I share what I claim as a cultural heritage. I share in kind, though perhaps not in degree, some of their material realities. I do not share their time or place. I have known, for example, the oppression and domination of the segregated South, but not slavery or Reconstruction. I write about northern, mostly urban woman, and I grew up in the rural South. I recognize the important cultural resonances that exist across African diasporic communities, but I understand also the existence of dissonance, especially as these distinctions become complicated by the passage of time and by cross-cultural fusions that I have experienced, and which they may have experienced differently. (271–72)

Royster's close attention to the contexts of her own life and the lives of her subjects is crucial to what she calls "afrafeminist" research, which aims to create knowledge that is informative to and representative of the group whose lives are studied (275). As she writes, "We speak and interpret *with* the community, not just *for* the community, or *about* the community" (275). Consequently, as someone who is positioned both as an academic and as a member of the community for whom she researches, she aims to "establish a sense of reciprocity between [her] two homes," knowing that this negotiation is complex and ongoing (254).

Ellen Cushman enacts a similarly reflexive approach to herself as researcher in her study, *The Struggle and the Tools: Oral and Literate Strategies in an Inner City Community*, which explores the language practices of community members in an African-American, inner city neighborhood. Like Royster, Cushman makes visible the inside-outside position she holds as an activist researcher, occupying both points of intersection with and differences from community residents. "Even though I was a graduate student in a prestigious private university, my class standing went from working class, when my folks were married, to White trash, when they divorced and we were evicted" (241). These intersections mattered when Mirena, a community member, received an eviction notice and requested that Cushman help her "sound right" in approaching prospective landlords. Together they role-played a conversation with the landlord and developed a statement that would help Mirena explain her reasons for moving. As Cushman describes it, "She saw me as an institutional representative who not only knew how to speak White, but was also getting a degree in English to become a broker of the linguistic code she now needed" (30). At the same time, Cushman's exchanges with Mirena helped her better understand how Mirena "troubleshoots and redefines her linguistic strategies necessary in order to get ahead" (30).

Both Royster and Cushman reject the idea of the objective, disembodied researcher, and instead enact research that relies on illumination of the researcher's multiple social locations, histories, and goals; this awareness of difference also altered the way feminist scholars advocated for use of experience in the classroom. For instance, in her 1998 essay "Reading and Writing Differences: The Problematic of Experience," Lu warns that in "validating the authority of the personal," we must also be "vigilant toward the tendency to invoke experience as an inherent right that erases differences along lines of race, class, gender, or sexual identity. We need to imagine ways of using experience critically: Experience should motivate us to care about another's differences and should disrupt the material conditions that gave rise to it" (436). Lu notes that her own female students are often invested in critiquing gender inequity, but don't always attend to how sexism is interlaced with other forms of oppression. Ultimately, she argues for reading, writing, and revision assignments that prompt students to articulate, and then reflect on and revise, their experiences by examining how they are shaped by interlocking issues of race, class, sexual identity, and gender.

Ritchie offers another example of a pedagogy that values women's experience as a resource for knowledge, and at the same time, insists upon a complex conception of women's subjectivity. As a participant-observer in colleague Barbara DiBernard's Women in Literature class, she notes how Barbara "tried to create opportunities for students to connect their lives to the readings and to connect both to action" ("Confronting" 97). That is, the students not only engaged a range of texts by writers who occupy diverse and complex identities but they also engaged one another in ways that brought students "face to face with alternate perspectives" and "challenged students [. . .] to reexamine their values and assumptions about women's lives" (95). Ritchie's interviews with students indicate that this learning was not always comfortable or tension-free, but it was, in the end, powerful. As one student wrote, "Of course I have a better understanding of woman authors, but I also see growth in myself and more understanding of other people" (99). Like Lu's pedagogy, then, students moved beyond simply giving voice to their own experiences as women to instead placing that experience within a cultural context and alongside the experience of other women. While this pedagogy often prompted important individual growth for students, it also encouraged social action. To connect the course to action, Barbara began each class with announcements about campus and community events related to their readings, requiring them to attending at least two such events and to connect them through writing to their readings. As Ritchie notes, she demonstrated and fostered a responsibility tied to responsiveness to the needs of others (97).

In both feminist research and classroom practice, then, attention to social location and experience began as, and remains, an important resource for knowledge. This approach to experiential knowledge also promotes a revised academic persona that values social location, experience, and particularity. As feminists added new lenses to their visions of gender and social inequities, their focus increasingly sharpened on responsibility to others, attention to difference, and social change. As I show in the next chapter, this resulted in a range of new questions about conceptions of academic writing, including what it means to approach argument through a feminist lens.

For Writing and Discussion

1. How have you been invited, as a researcher or writer, to draw upon your experience as knowledge? What was the effect of your doing so? Was it taken as seriously as traditional research?

2. What would it mean to enact rigorous reflexivity about your position as researcher or writer?

Works Cited

Annas, Pamela J. "Style as Politics: A Feminist Approach to the Teaching of Writing." *Feminism and Composition: A Critical Sourcebook*. Ed. Gesa E. Kirsch et al. Boston, MA: Bedford/St. Martin's, 2003. 61–72. Print.

Belenky, Mary Field et al. *Women's Ways of Knowing: The Development of Self, Voice, and Mind*. New York: Basic Books, 1986. Print.

Chodorow, Nancy. *The Reproduction of Mothering: Psychoanalysis and the Sociology of Gender*. Berkeley: U of California P, 1978. Print.

Cushman, Ellen. *The Struggle and the Tools: Oral and Literate Strategies in an Inner City Community*. Albany: SUNY P, 1998. Print.

Flynn, Elizabeth A. "Composing as a Woman." *Feminism and Composition: A Critical Sourcebook*. Ed. Gesa E. Kirsch et al. Boston, MA: Bedford/St. Martin's, 2003. 243–55. Print.

—. "Contextualizing 'Composing as a Woman.'" *Feminism and Composition: A Critical Sourcebook*. Ed. Gesa E. Kirsch et al. Boston, MA: Bedford/St. Martin's, 2003. 339–41. Print.

Gilligan, Carol. *In a Different Voice: Psychological Theory in Women's Development*. Cambridge, MA: Harvard UP, 1982. Print.

Howe, Florence. "Identity and Expression: A Writing Course for Women." *Feminism and Composition: A Critical Sourcebook*. Ed. Gesa E. Kirsch et al. Boston, MA: Bedford/St. Martin's, 2003. 33–42. Print.

Lu, Min-Zhan. "Reading and Writing Differences: The Problematic of Experience." *Feminism and Composition: A Critical Sourcebook.* Ed. Gesa E. Kirsch et al. Boston, MA: Bedford/St. Martin's, 2003. 436–46. Print.

Ritchie, Joy S. "Confronting the 'Essential' Problem: Reconnecting Feminist Theory and Pedagogy." *Feminism and Composition: A Critical Sourcebook.* Ed. Gesa E. Kirsch et al. Boston, MA: Bedford/St. Martin's, 2003. 79–102. Print.

Ritchie, Joy S., and Gesa E. Kirsch. "Beyond the Personal: Theorizing a Politics of Location in Composition Research." *Feminism and Composition: A Critical Sourcebook.* Ed. Gesa E. Kirsch et al. Boston, MA: Bedford/St. Martin's, 2003. 140–59. Print.

Royster, Jacqueline Jones. *Traces of a Stream: Literacy and Social Change Among African American Women.* Pittsburgh, PA: U of Pittsburgh P, 2000. Print.

Sullivan, Patricia A. "Feminism and Methodology in Composition Studies." *Feminism and Composition: A Critical Sourcebook.* Ed. Gesa E. Kirsch et al. Boston, MA: Bedford/St. Martin's, 2003. 124–39. Print.

For Further Reading

Brodkey, Linda. "Writing on the Bias." *College English* 56.5 (1994): 527–48. Print.

Duran, Jane. *Philosophies of Science/Feminist Theories.* Boulder, CO: Westview, 1998. Print.

Foss, Karen A., and Sonja K. Foss. "Personal Experience as Evidence in Feminist Scholarship." *Western Journal of Communication* 58.1 (1994): 39–43. Print.

Schell, Eileen. *Rhetorica in Motion: Feminist Rhetorical Methods and Methodologies.* Pittsburgh, PA: U of Pittsburgh P, 2010. Print.

Spigelman, Candace. "Argument and Evidence in the Case of the Personal." *College English* 64.1 (2001): 63–87. Print.

Surman Paley, Karen. *I Writing: The Politics and Practice of Teaching First-Person Writing.* Carbondale: Southern Illinois UP, 2001. Print.

6 Argument Through a Feminist Lens

If you turn on CNN, read a column in the newspaper, or attend an academic lecture, chances are, you're likely to encounter monologic arguments that seek to persuade you, to prompt you to change your mind. Communication scholar Richard L. Johannesen characterizes the monologic argument in these terms: "A person employing monologue seeks to command, coerce, manipulate, conquer, dazzle, deceive, or exploit. Other persons are viewed as 'things' to be exploited solely for the communicator's self-serving purpose" (69). While Johannesen's definition cannot be applied to all persuasive speech and writing, it may not seem far-reaching when we consider the arguments featured on our twenty-four-hour news cycles among political pundits or even between our political leaders, vying for votes at election time.

Within the academy, the monologic argument is also the normative mode of discourse—a value we can trace back to western classical rhetoric, where persuasion and victory was considered the primary purpose of public speech acts. As Gerald Graff and Cathy Birkenstein observe in their popular textbook *They Say/I Say: The Moves that Matter in Academic Writing*, "Broadly speaking, academic writing is argumentative writing" (3). As the title of their book suggests, however, they do insist that the academic argument is part of an ongoing conversation. Even so, how they describe the role of others' contributions is telling. They write, "We believe that to argue well you need to more than assert your own ideas. You need to enter a conversation, using what others say (or might say) as a launching pad or sounding board for your own ideas" (3). Here, then, we see the normative approach to others' ideas within academic argument: as a means to promoting one's own perspective.

Chapter 6: Argument Through a Feminist Lens

In what follows, I show how feminists in composition help us to see that while the monologic, persuasive argument is the valued model of discourse in our universities and our wider culture, it is not the only way of going about our work. They argue for and enact collaborative processes that make visible the social nature of writing and show how creativity flourishes through dialogue. Feminist scholars also attend to the role of listener in new ways, arguing for listening as a vital, active process that is required not only for new voices to be heard but for genuine dialogue to take place.

Persuasion, Conflict, and Negotiation Through a Feminist Lens

"In the real world," Graff and Birkenstein argue, "we don't make arguments without being provoked. We make arguments because someone has said or done something [. . .] and we need to respond. [. . .] If it weren't for other people and our need to challenge, agree with, or otherwise respond to them, there would be no reason to argue at all" (3–4). Indeed, their characterization of argument represents the dominant model: We argue to move someone from their side to our side.

Feminists, however, point to some of the problems with persuasion as privileged discourse. For instance, in her 1979 article "The Womanization of Rhetoric," Sally Miller Gearhart makes an early feminist call to rethink academic argument's construction as combative and conquest-focused (53). She writes, "The patriarchs of rhetoric have never called into question their unspoken assumption that mankind (read 'mankind') is here on earth to alter his (read 'his') environment and to influence the social affairs of other men (read 'men')" (53). Gearhart's concern is that when rhetoric is conceived only as a means to change another, communication is one-directional, with the speaker/writer persuading and the listener converting. She likens this to problematic gender hierarchies, where all the power rests in the masculine speaker, and the feminized listener simply receives or yields to his sway (58).

Gearhart proposes an alternative model, which favors communication over persuasion and makes room for mutual change. This, she argues, is a model steeped in feminist principle: "Feminism is at the very least the rejection of the conquest/conversion model of interaction and the development of new forms of relationship which allow for wholeness in the individual and differences among people and entities" (59).

For this to occur, she insists that the dynamics of dialogue change, such that both parties seek to create an atmosphere of learning. Even when power differences exist, the participants need to "feel equal in power to each other," and each needs to exhibit willingness to yield his or her position (57). She also proposes that such a shift in dynamics has the potential to change learning. Whereas the teacher is usually positioned as the knower who ultimately changes students with her knowledge, she suggests the teacher must also "prepare to be changed with students in the mutually created setting" (57). Indeed, in the proposal Gearhart offers for feminist dialogue, you may hear echoes of the calls by Florence Howe and Pamela J. Annas for feminist writing classrooms described in the last chapter; each of these feminist thinkers sought to illuminate and alter cultural and institutional norms in order to make these situations more hospitable to alternative modes of knowing and being.

Writing just over a decade later in 1991, Catherine E. Lamb's "Beyond Argument in Feminist Composition" provides an oft-cited call for feminist alternatives to the "monologic argument" (283). The monologic argument is, she notes, the way most of us learned to construct arguments: "what we want comes first, and we use the available means of persuasion to get it, in, one hopes, ethical ways. We may acknowledge the other side's position but only to refute it" (283). For Lamb, a central problem with this model is that it presumes conflict can be removed by a one-sided effort; change or resolution will materialize as a result of advancing the best, or strongest, argument.

Instead, Lamb posits negotiation and mediation as an alternative to argument, such that the goal "is no longer to win but to arrive at a solution that is acceptable to both sides" (288). At least two key assumptions drive her proposition. First, she views power not as something one party holds and "uses" on another but as something that can be shared and employed by both participants in the dialogue. Rather than promoting arguments where a writer crafts and hones a position, she seeks to offer students opportunities to collaborate (even as arguing different positions might be part of that process) on negotiating a mutually agreeable solution. This is the second assumption central to Lamb's vision: a focus on positions will only lead to deeper entrenchment into those locations. Instead, she advocates for identifying interests or issues as a way to locate common ground and to increase the "space between the two parties, making it possible for the distance

Chapter 6: Argument Through a Feminist Lens   87

between them to lessen as they move toward each other" (288). Here, you might notice a trace of Mary Astell's seventeenth-century efforts to advocate for the use of inquiry toward "truth" rather than mere "victory," or Margaret Fuller's work in the 1800s to replace dualistic argument with multivocal dialogue.

In order to depict the pedagogical possibilities of this position, Lamb draws from her own teaching. She describes an assignment in which students work in groups of three to negotiate a problem of their choosing. Two students assume one "side" in the debate, and the third student acts as the mediator. Through role-playing, memo writing, and discussion, the mediator gathers as full a picture as possible from both sides and then involves the other two students in coming up with possible options toward a solution. The end goal of the assignment is to come up with an agreeable solution to both parties. As Lamb notes, "Argument still has a place, although now as a means, not an end" (281).

In the first-year writing program at my institution, whose curriculum features argument, our TAs often struggle with how to move students beyond a rigid conception of argument as a two-sided debate, with persuasion as the primary goal. To help the first-year students listen to multiple voices and perspectives, many of the TAs draw from the example offered by graduate student Amber Harris Leichner in our program's *TA Sourcebook*. This assignment aims to complicate the very notion of argument by emphasizing its multiplicity. In one part of this three-prong series, Leichner invites her students to challenge a polarizing position by taking an "integrative stance." The student selects an issue often deemed polarizing and researches its multiple sides in order to integrate perspectives. She suggests that students ask the following questions about the people who hold polarizing positions about the chosen issue: What do they believe? What are their basic assumptions about the issue? What is their history in relation to the issue? What are their goals, fears, and passions? What language do they use to "frame" the issue?

Leichner then moves students into a related project, inviting them to imagine a dialogue around a table or at a board meeting, whereby participants propose distinct and multiple positions. She asks the students to compose proposals, deliberately examining the issue from a range of perspectives and showing readers "that each proposal deserves careful consideration." Then, the student is to propose a solution that the majority of the group might accept. The goal is to discover a space of shared ground, even among diverse positions.

Not all feminist scholars agree that a turn away from persuasive discourse or conflict is productive. Most notably, Susan C. Jarratt's 1991 (the same year as Lamb's) article "Feminism and Composition: The Case for Conflict," argues that without an ability to engage in conflict and make strong arguments, students are insufficiently prepared "to negotiate the oppressive discourses of racism, sexism, and classism surfacing in the composition classroom" (264). For Jarratt, conflict is inevitable in classes that foreground student knowledge because students' experiences are necessarily situated in complex social and political circumstances that result in inequalities. In fact, she challenges Gearhart's idea that two participants can "feel equal in power to each other," offering an example of a black student in an all white class, who may never feel equity in that setting (265). On the other hand, recognizing the inevitability of conflict, Jarratt notes, "is not grounds for despair" (275). Instead, she views conflict as a resource for exploration—"a starting point for creating a consciousness in students and teachers through which the inequalities generating those conflicts can be acknowledged and transformed" (276). Jarratt recommends, then, that teachers help students to understand that what may look and feel like individual conflicts are tied to social and historical contexts, and these contexts deserve analysis and discussion that may well take place through "heated argument" (278).

Ultimately, Jarratt calls for a rhetorical approach to argument—attendant to context, purpose, audience—indicating that there are times when advancing non-conflict and negotiation can be productive and times when it can be debilitating (272). For instance, she notes that "advising a female student to 'swallow' without reply a conventional male reaction to a woman's experience has serious consequences" (268), and she further insists that there are indeed times when feminists do need to make forceful, authoritative arguments. Consequently, she strives to offer female students and teachers a greater range of possible options for engaging conflict. While she wants students to "identify their personal interests with others [and] understand those interests" as socially implicated, also of primary import to Jarratt is that students advance these interests in "a public voice"—something long denied to women, as our rhetorical history makes clear (277). In the next section, I point to the ways feminists complicate and extend traditional notions of "voice" in academic discourse.

For Writing and Discussion

1. Our media is saturated with examples of two-sided, persuasion-driven debate. What examples can you find of dialogue where mediation, not persuasion, is the goal? How is the process of discussion, information-gathering, presenting of knowledge, etc. changed as a result?

2. Can you think of current issues in which you are invested where mediation or negotiation would not be an option? On the other hand, can you think of public issues or debates where parties are locked in their positions in ways that make neither persuasion nor mediation possible?

Beyond the Monologic Voice

For feminist scholars, one of the central problems with academic (indeed, cultural) discourse is the seemingly singular and monologic voice it privileges. That is, as Andrea Abernethy Lunsford and Lisa Ede note, our society locates "power, authority, authenticity, and property in an autonomous, masculine self" ("Rhetoric" 267). This construction is stubbornly present in academic writing, even as poststructuralist theory insists that meaning is as much dependent on what the reader brings to the text as on what the author intended.

Feminists point to and challenge (at least) two central problems with this conception of the authorial voice. First, emphasis on a singular, autonomous author disguises the social nature of writing—that is, even in "single-authored" texts, the writer has, in nearly every case, been influenced directly and indirectly by a plethora of other voices. Second, as Lunsford notes, our culture tends to conflate authorship with property, such that it is easiest to assume one "owns" a text if she or he is the only author. This, she contends, is why there is "academic suspicion" of cooperative work ("Rhetoric, Feminism" 181); those evaluating the value of the text wonder, "Whose is it, really?" Lunsford further reminds us that our culture's obsession with the "author" of intellectual property has "disenfranchised many, many creators—a great many of whom are women" (181). Indeed, women, long denied opportunities to act as authors, have made important but unacknowledged contributions to the work of men. Recall, for instance, that as I describe in Chapter 2, scholars now believe Aspasia was the writer of the famous funeral oration in Plato's *Menexenus*; while his speech is remembered, she presumably composed the words he spoke. Additionally, women's collaborative, creative contributions have also long existed but gone unnoticed because they fell outside of the traditional public, persuasive realm of rhetoric. In order to illuminate the importance of collaborative inquiry and composing, scholars like Lunsford and Ede have dedicated significant scholarly efforts to studying and advocating for collaborative authorship, or multivocal texts—which they call rhetoric in a "new key."

In their article "Rhetoric in a New Key: Women and Collaboration" and their book *Singular Texts/Plural Authors: Perspectives on Collaborative Writing*, Lunsford and Ede discuss their findings based on a study of collaborative writers in seven disciplines. While they note that collaborative dynamics are necessarily shaped by political, social, and ideological contexts, they found two primary modes of collaboration. The first is a "hierarchical mode," which positions one contributor (usually the most senior person) as the lead author and operates from a linear structure, and highly specific, predetermined goals ("Rhetoric" 257). Knowledge, in this model, is perceived as "information to be found" or a "problem to be solved," and productivity and efficiency are highly valued (257). Because this is a mode of collaborative writing that does not disrupt authorial hierarchy or knowledge production—in fact, it reifies monologic discourse—they label it a "predominantly masculine mode" (257). Indeed, when my students express resistance to collaborative projects, it is often because their experiences of collaboration reflect this mode: One person leads and the others follow (or worse, remain disengaged).

In contrast, Lunsford and Ede promote "dialogic discourse," which positions writers' roles as fluid—that is, the writers occupy "multiple and shifting roles" as the writing process ensues (257). While the collaborators work toward goals, the process of developing, discussing, and revising the project is as important as the end result. Additionally, dialogic collaborators acknowledge the creative tension inherent in such projects and value these moments as opportunities for reflection—much in the way Jarratt approaches conflict as a resource for discovery and inquiry. Dialogic collaboration, then, challenges single-authored, monologic texts and seeks to establish authorship as grounded in collaborative, relational acts (261). They point to Anne Ruggles Gere's study of women's writing groups and Jacqueline Jones Royster's accounting of black women writers (see Chapter 3) as illustrations of dialogical collaboration.

In the years that followed Lunsford and Ede's call for rhetoric in a "new key," a plethora of collaboratively written texts emerged. In fact, in her 1997 opinion piece in *College English*, Gesa E. Kirsch classifies the emergence of multivocal texts as "a new force in composition studies" (192). She chronicles a list of texts that involve collaboration not only between composition scholars but also between professors and graduate students, professors and undergraduates, and in one case, a compositionist and her mother (a kindergarten teacher) (192). These projects accomplish a range of work; they illuminate the dialogic nature of writing; make visible how students contribute to the knowledge of Composition Studies; and disrupt the form of the monologic argument. For instance, Jill Eichhorn, Sara Farris, Karen Hayes, Adriana Hernández, Susan C. Jarratt, Karen Powers-Stubbs, and Marian M. Sciachitano offer a multivocal "symposium," whose form reflects the writers' bi-weekly feminist discussion group. Their piece allows them to speak "as a collective" in their "seven different voices," which reflect differences in race, class, age, education background, and institutional status. Each provides a narrative that reflects not only personal experience but also depicts how that experience has been re-understood as a result of their collective dialogue.

In addition to writing collaboratively, feminist scholars also use alternative forms and media to illuminate the multiplicity of the single voice. In some cases, this involves a writer moving between or melding voices that represent different aspects of her subjectivity. In "Re-composing as a Woman—An Essay in Different Voices," Terry Myers Zawacki melds personal writing about gardening, academic readings, and reflections on scholarly texts and teaching. She asks:

> Is it possible to challenge the traditional academic hierarchy which privileges expository prose by rejecting the distinction between personal writing? By showing that genre boundaries and that all writing is a means of creating a self, not for expressing a self that already exists? If I situate myself in the context

> of other voices, if I write about experiences and feelings, if I choose not to get to the point, it's not because I am a woman, but rather because I want to discover the possibilities of representing a gendered self in writing. (319)

Rather than crafting a precise, singular voice that funnels to a clear argument (or, as she writes, "get[s] to the point"), she merges her multiple voices so as to build toward an opening, a set of questions to prompt the field's further growth.

In another effort to promote multivocal discourse, Julie Jung argues for the use of "multigenre" texts. She defines this form as "experimental scholarly essays that are marked by the conscious juxtaposition of academic essay with other genres, including poetry, fiction, creative nonfiction, and drama" (33). (Indeed, Fuller's work described in Chapter 2 might well be considered an early example of this genre.) In Jung's book *Revisionary Rhetoric, Feminist Pedagogy and Multigenre Texts*, she offers a multigenre epilogue, which includes scholarly analysis, personal reflection on her work as a writer, scholar, and teacher, as well as poetry. Jung notes that one significant mark of the multigenre essay is the use of white space to separate the genres; the space is itself meaningful, leaving room for silence, reflection, and disruption.

We can also locate possibilities for multivocal texts in a much more predominant form: online hypertext. In their 1999 essay "Writing Multiplicity: Hypertext and Feminist Textual Politics," Donna LeCourt and LuAnn Barnes point out that hypertext challenges the assumptions that a text must have a unified voice. The problem with the singular voice privileged in academic discourse, they contend, is that it requires students to construct "masculine textual selves," and to "silence feminist perspectives that might contradict such unity" (323–24). Alternatively, allowing students to construct multivocal hypertext, they suggest, is a way to highlight—to readers and to the writer, herself—the contradictory, multiple, fluid range of positions each of us occupies, and in so doing, to open a range of discursive possibilities.

Because multivocal, multigenre texts challenge notions of linear, progressive argument, a demand is placed on readers to likewise shift their practices. Jung writes, "Revisionary rhetors seek to disrupt their readers' harmonious reading experiences by using textual strategies that delay immediate convergence of meaning" (34). Readers, then, are not allowed to simply "consume" texts in a way that is familiar;

instead, they must move through disruptions, shifts, and unexpected connections, and ultimately, participate with the text to create meaning.

Even as feminist scholars carve new possibilities for constructing and representing dialogic or multivocal scholarship, they also guard against pure celebration of these news forms. LeCourt and Barnes observe, for instance, that their "practical experience as authors of hypertext tempers an unqualified celebration of its theoretical potential" (322). In her opinion piece on multivocal texts, Kirsch warns of some potential limitations of these forms. Collaboratively-written texts with a range of writers, she notes, can obscure the power dynamics that necessarily shape the writing process: "Such strategies [. . .] often serve only to make authors appear equal on the page while they actually disguise important social and cultural differences" (195). In addition, while scholars like Jung celebrate the new requirements multivocal texts place on readers, Kirsch fears that they might become "elitist and exclusionary" (194). Ultimately, she does not suggest moving away from such texts, but calls for great reflexivity about when, why, and how we employ such forms. Indeed, her critique points to a concern that shapes all texts that break discursive norms: Will it be heard?

This brings me to yet another important way feminist scholars in Composition Studies have disrupted monologic discourse—by attending to listening.

For Writing and Discussion

1. In their 1990 article "Rhetoric in a New Key: Women and Collaboration," Lunsford and Ede offer several examples that depict the power of the single-author construct. Here are three:

   A prestigious English department decided to withdraw its undergraduate prize when the anonymous "author" of the winning poem turned out to be three undergraduate collaborators.

   Two women who petitioned and were granted permission to conduct collaborative research on a dissertation project were later told they would have to produce two separate and "different" dissertations.

> At a large research institution, a woman who often writes collaboratively was tenured and promoted to associate professor—but warned that her promotion to full professor would be contingent on producing single-authored books and articles. (259)

> What do you see at stake in each of these situations? What does each tell us about the institution's assumption about knowledge? Collaboration? Authorship?

2. How many opportunities have you had in your educational history to collaborate? On what kind of assignment was this allowed? When was it not allowed? How do you make sense of this distinction? How did your collaborative learning experience compare to those in which you worked individually?

Rhetorical Listening

For writers like Gearhart and Jung, new practices of argument also require new attention to listening. As Jung writes, "the challenge for revisionary rhetors [. . .] is to produce heteroglossic discourse that both listens well as it makes itself heard" (33). However, in order to do so, we need to go back and consider how and why we listen to others within academic discourse. Graff and Birkenstein note that "the underlying structure of academic writing—and of responsible public discourse—resides not just in stating our own ideas but in listening closely to others around us" (3). While we may teach students to start with what "they say" or to do the "background reading," the aims of such a practice are not necessarily the same as fostering an ability to *listen* to the scholarly dialogue they engage. Recall Lamb's quotation cited earlier: "We may acknowledge the other side's position but only to refute it" (283).

Feminist scholars, therefore, have sought to challenge traditional notions of listening and to reclaim it as a crucial rhetorical trope necessary for genuine dialogue. In her groundbreaking 1999 article "Rhetorical Listening: A Trope for Interpretive Invention and a 'Code of Cross-Cultural Conduct'," Krista Ratcliffe prompts the field to revitalize its attention to listening as a rhetorical practice. As Composition Studies has recovered rhetoric, she observes that writing and reading serve as the two dominant tropes for invention, followed by speech,

Chapter 6: Argument Through a Feminist Lens 95

with listening running a "poor, poor fourth" (195). Ratcliffe traces this devaluing of listening to cultural (mis)conceptions of the rhetorical term *logos*. According to Martin Heidegger, the west inherited *logos* as the Greek noun, understood as a system of reasoning and forming logic, but lost its verb form, *legein*, which means not only to speak but also "to lay down, to lay before"—that is, to listen (Heidegger, qtd. in Fiumara 3). The result is an impoverished notion of language that relies on an "arrogant" logos, ignoring knowledge deemed "irrational" or "illogical" (Fiumara 6). In addition to excluding particular kinds of voices, *logos* without listening also perpetuates a homogenized mode of speech based on competition rather than dialogue. Or, as Wayne C. Booth puts it, a rhetoric that overvalues the question of "How can I change your mind?" and undervalues that of "When should I change my mind?" (Booth and Elbow 379). Indeed, Ratcliffe observes that the traditional habit of academic reading is to discern "what we can agree with or challenge" (203). How, in other words, can I use this text to serve my own argument?

Listening is also devalued within popular culture, where it is naturalized as something we all do but no one needs to study (Ratcliffe 196). One reason for the low status listening occupies, Ratcliffe contends, is its association with the "feminine"; that is, historically, listening serves as the passive counterpart to speech, signifying deference, support, or courtesy. Drawing upon Deborah Tannen's study of listening and gender, Ratcliffe summarizes: "Men are socialized to play the listening game via the questions 'Have I won?' and 'Do you respect me?' while women are socialized to play it via the questions 'Have I been helpful?' and 'Do you like me?'" (200). Listening as deference is also evident if we consider who has been historically positioned as listener—so as to follow orders or to discern how to "fit in" to dominant culture—and who has occupied the position of speaker.

In order to reach beyond naturalized approaches to listening and logos, Ratcliffe proposes an alternative concept: rhetorical listening. Rhetorical listening stems from a restored logos, whose aim is not to improve the prospects for the individual success of the hearer but instead to alter the dynamics of argument and dialogue in a way that emphasizes reflection, responsibility, and understanding of difference. To listen rhetorically is to assume a deliberate stance centered upon "a capacity and willingness" to situate oneself openly in relation to discourse, whether written, spoken, or imagistic (Ratcliffe 204). In this way, one could rhetorically listen to a printed text as well as the spoken word.

Part of achieving this stance involves listening *with* intent, which she names "standing under"—an inversion of understanding. Standing under a text means listening with the intent to acknowledge both the cultural logics and (fluid) standpoints that inform another's discourses *and* those that inform our own (205).

For instance, a person striving to listen rhetorically might ask: What social locations do I indentify with most strongly in my life? How do those locations inform how I listen? What do they help me to listen to more closely? What might they prohibit me from hearing? Of course, cultural logics shape our individual positions, so one may also consider what cultural belief systems (national, community, family, etc.) inform his or her individual responses to the text. The aim is not to for the listener to reject or overcome the social locations and positions she or he occupies but to increase awareness about how they, often without our awareness, seep into our engagement with others' ideas.

One of the teachers in our first-year composition program, Jessica Rivera-Mueller, has integrated rhetorical listening into her instruction as a way to help students engage difficult texts. Drawing from Ratcliffe, she begins by showing students a list of tendencies many of us employ when listening: 1) appropriating: taking someone's ideas to support our own; 2) identifying: pointing to connections of either agreement or disagreement; 3) defending: entering a discussion only to challenge a perspective rather than to engage it in dialogue. She then offers an alternative list comprised of the practices of rhetorical listening: 1) engaging another voice to seek deeper understanding of ourselves and others; 2) being accountable for our own positions and logics or assumptions; 3) analyzing the cultural logics that shape the text's claims. To help them enact rhetorical listening, Rivera-Mueller invites them into a discussion of "All's Not Well in Land of 'The Lion King,'" a critical movie review by Margaret Lazarus. She notes that many students are resistant to this text, which critiques a favorite childhood film. As they discuss the text, they try to move away from the normative listening practices to instead practice rhetorical listening. Indeed, this is difficult, complex work, and it involves practicing something we have not commonly learned to do, but Jessica notes that it helps to give students a vocabulary for listening and to establish practices they can continue to develop together.

Because feminist attention to listening requires mindfulness of power dynamics at play in listening and speaking situations, Ratcliffe concedes that there are indeed times when possibilities for rhetorical listening to others do not exist. Ratcliffe puts it this way: "We learn by listening to those who do not agree with us, provided the listening occurs in the context of 'genuine conversation' (Copeland), where there is a desire in all parties to move our understanding forward" (212). If we are attentive to power dynamics, however, and alert to the ways that difference teaches even when agreement is not possible, feminist scholars like Ratcliffe suggest that rhetorical listening can help foster not only richer dialogue but also deeper understanding of the possibilities and limitations of our positions.

FOR WRITING AND DISCUSSION

1. What commitments, positions, and/or aspects of your identity shape how you listen? What kinds of arguments are you most open to hearing? To what (or whom) is it difficult for you to listen? Why might it be useful to consider the intentions and locations that affect your listening?

2. At the K-12 level, listening skills are part of English language arts standards in thirty-eight states, which means listening, in those states, is now a skill for which students (and teachers) are held accountable by the No Child Left Behind Act. Here listening is typically understood as comprehension of oral material in the classroom, with evidence of good listening associated with memory and attention. How did you learn listening as a student? How do traditional conceptions of listening differ from feminist rhetorical listening?

FROM MONOLOGIC TO DIALOGIC: A FEMINIST REVISION OF ARGUMENT

In order to assert their voices and perspectives, to challenge masculine norms, and to offer alternative values and practices, feminists have had to make strong arguments. It probably isn't surprising that as they undertake the complex work of social change, there is disagreement among feminist scholars about the role of conflict, mediation, and persuasion within argument. Where they come together, however, is in the act of highlighting the way categories we often take for granted as natural and fixed—like argument and academic writing—are in fact social constructs that can be revised. What if, feminist scholars prompt us to ask, we approach academic argument not with an intention to change others but with a responsibility to others? What if the purpose of argument were not to deliver a predetermined position but to inquire into an issue in order to discover its multiple, often conflicting, facets? What if we attended to others' insights not to agree or disagree but to help us reconsider our own positions? By posing questions that ripple the surface of normative academic practices, feminist scholars expand the range of what counts as knowledge, how we produce and share it, and who is considered a knower.

WORKS CITED

Booth, Wayne C., and Peter Elbow. "Symposium: The Limits and Alternatives to Skepticism: A Dialogue." *College English* 67.4 (2005): 378–99. Print.

Eichhorn, Jill, Sara Farris, Karen Hayes, Adriana Hernandez, Susan C. Jarratt, Karen Powers-Stubbs, and Marian M. Sciachitano. "A Symposium on Feminist Experience in the Composition Classroom." *College Composition and Communication* 43.3 (1992): 297–322. Print.

Fiumara, Gemma Corradi. *The Other Side of Language: A Philosophy of Listening.* London: Routledge, 1990. Print.

Gearhart, Sally Miller. "The Womanization of Rhetoric." *Feminism and Composition: A Critical Sourcebook.* Ed. Gesa E. Kirsch et al. Boston, MA: Bedford/St. Martin's, 2003. 53–60. Print.

Graff, Gerald, and Cathy Birkenstein. *They Say/I Say: The Moves that Matter in Academic Writing.* New York: W. W. Norton & Company, Inc., 2006. Print.

Jarratt, Susan C. "Feminism and Composition: A Case for Conflict." *Feminism and Composition: A Critical Sourcebook.* Ed. Gesa E. Kirsch et al. Boston, MA: Bedford/St. Martin's, 2003. 263–80. Print.

Johannesen, Richard L. *Ethics in Human Communication.* 4th ed. Prospect Heights, IL: Waveland Press, 1996. Print.

Jung, Julie. *Revisionary Rhetoric, Feminist Pedagogy, and Multigenre Texts.* Carbondale: Southern Illinois UP 2005. Print.

Kirsch, Gesa E. "Multi-Vocal Texts and Interpretive Responsibility." *College English* 59.2: 1997 (191–202). Print.

Lamb, Catherine E. "Beyond Argument in Feminist Composition." *Feminism and Composition: A Critical Sourcebook*. Ed. Gesa E. Kirsch et al. Boston, MA: Bedford/St. Martin's, 2003. 281–93. Print.

LeCourt, Donna, and Luann Barnes. "Writing Multiplicity: Hypertext and Feminist Textual Politics." *Feminism and Composition: A Critical Sourcebook*. Ed. Gesa E. Kirsch et al. Boston, MA: Bedford/St. Martin's, 2003. 321–38. Print.

Leichner, Amber Harris. *TA Sourcebook*. U of Nebraska, Lincoln: 2008.

Lunsford, Andrea Abernethy. "Rhetoric, Feminism, and the Politics of Textual Ownership." *Feminism and Composition: A Critical Sourcebook*. Ed. Gesa E. Kirsch et al. Boston, MA: Bedford/St. Martin's, 2003. 180–93. Print.

Lunsford, Andrea, and Lisa Ede. *Singular Texts/Plural Authors: Perspectives on Collaborative Writing*. Carbondale: Southern Illinois UP, 1990. Print.

Lunsford, Andrea Abernethy, and Lisa Ede. "Rhetoric in a New Key: Women and Collaboration." *Feminism and Composition: A Critical Sourcebook*. Ed. Gesa E. Kirsch et al. Boston, MA: Bedford/St. Martin's, 2003. 256–62. Print.

Ratcliffe, Krista. "Rhetorical Listening: A Trope for Interpretive Invention and a 'Code of Cross-Cultural Conduct'." *College Composition and Communication* 51.2 (1999): 195–224. Print.

Zawacki, Terry Myers. "Recomposing as a Woman—An Essay in Different Voices." *Feminism and Composition: A Critical Sourcebook*. Ed. Gesa E. Kirsch et al. Boston, MA: Bedford/St. Martin's, 2003. 314–20. Print.

For Further Reading

Glenn, Cheryl, and Krista Ratcliffe, eds. *Silence and Listening as Rhetorical Arts*. Carbondale: Southern Illinois UP, 2011. Print.

kynard, carmen. "'New Life in This Dormant Creature': Notes on Social Consciousness, Language, and Learning in a College Classroom." *Alt Dis: Alternative Discourses and the Academy*. Ed. Christopher Schroeder, Helen Fox, and Patricia Bizzell. Portsmouth, NH: Boynton/Cook Heinemann, 2002. 31–44. Print.

Powell, Malea. "Listening to Ghosts: An Alternative (Non)Argument." *Alt Dis: Alternative Discourses and the Academy*. Ed. Christopher Schroeder, Helen Fox, and Patricia Bizzell. Portsmouth, NH: Boynton/Cook Heinemann, 2002. 11–22. Print.

Welch, Nancy. "Taking Sides." *Teaching Rhetorica: Theory, Pedagogy, Practice*. Ed. Kate Ronald and Joy Ritchie. Portsmouth, NH: Boynton/Cook Heinemann, 2006. 147–59. Print.

Epilogue

Last week in my graduate course on Composition Theory and Practice, my students reflected on how and when, in their history as learners, they came to see that the information presented to them in textbooks—from history to science—did not provide the "objective truth" of these fields, but was in fact a particular version of the story, articulated from a specific location and set of values. This realization didn't mean they should dismiss what they'd learned, but it did suggest that there were other versions of the stories, told from different perspectives, that they might investigate, and those alterative views might paint a more expansive, vivid picture of the story. This is what I hope this book has provided you: a feminist lens that broadens and complicates your view of Composition Studies.

One feature of a feminist lens is that it illuminates how gender functions in sites, practices, and knowledge, which, at first glance, might appear neutral. You've seen examples of this way of seeing throughout the book, from feminist historians characterizing the field of Composition Studies as feminized—and then seeking to alter those conditions—to feminist rhetoricians challenging traditional definitions of the rhetorical tradition that exclude women's voices.

A feminist lens does more, though, than illuminate masculinist perspectives or assumptions. It also helps to expand composition's field of vision, to extend what we're able to see. A feminist lens on composition's story, so far, has helped to train our attention on these issues and ideas:

- The *presence* of female voices and perspectives, ranging from ancient female rhetors to contemporary female students in our classrooms.
- The *difference* that exists among women, as one's experience of gender functions in interplay with class, race, sexual identity,

geography (among other locations), and how those differences shape the way we know, learn, and write.
- The *possibility* that comes with including new voices and different knowledge perspectives, changing how we conceive of rhetor, writer, teacher, and student; how we approach research, argument, and academic writing; and how we learn and teach the process of writing.

Perhaps the most significant characteristic of a feminist lens, though, is its focus on revision. As Adrienne Rich writes, "Re-vision—the act of looking back, of seeing with fresh eyes, of entering an old text from a new critical direction—is for women more than a chapter in cultural history: it is an act of survival" (35). A feminist lens, then, does not rest upon final answers or closure; instead, it invites reflection, rethinking, and rewriting, so that feminist knowledge, writing, and classrooms are ever-evolving. Whether we look back or into the future of Composition Studies, we can be sure that feminist scholars will continue to ask: Who is excluded? How is gender (and difference) accounted for? What is the purpose of learning, teaching, and writing? What can we learn from including new voices and perspectives, from students to community members to scholars?

Works Cited

Rich, Adrienne. *On Lies, Secrets, and Silence: Selected Prose 1966–1978*. New York: W. W. Norton & Company, Inc., 1979. Print.

Notes

1. While the phrase is best known as "Ain't I a Woman," scholars later pointed out that the speech was originally transcribed in a Southern dialect, which is not reflective of Truth's New York upbringing. Campbell edited the speech to remove the dialect, and I rely on her transcription.

2. The "first wave" of feminism is usually framed as the late nineteenth- and early twentieth-century efforts by women like the suffragists to procure the right to vote and to exert more public and political influence. The "second wave" emerged from the Civil Rights and anti-Vietnam War movement, beginning in the 1960s and lasting until the 1980s. During this time, women sought greater gender equity, including equal pay, reproductive rights, sexual freedom, and individual agency. Many feminists approached women as equal to, but still inherently different from, men, and thereby worked to celebrate those differences.

3. Trinh falls into the "third wave" of feminism (1990–current) when feminists complicated "essentialist" notions of gender, challenging the idea that there is an inherent "womanness" and instead promoting a postmodern conception of subjectivity, which holds that the self is made of multiple socially-constructed positions including race, class, sex, linguistic background, and so on. That is, gender is understood as shaped by culture, not (only) biologically determined. This wave also foregrounds differences within and within and among groups of women.

Index

academic argument, 15, 49, 84-85, 98
Annas, Pamela J., 73-74, 82, 86
Anthony, Susan B., 20, 31, 34-35, 38
Anzaldúa, Gloria, 42-43, 46-47, 49, 60, 73
Aristotle, 10, 20-23, 45
Aspasia, 20, 22-24, 32, 35-36, 38-39, 90
Astell, Mary, 28-29, 35-36, 46, 87

Barnes, LuAnn, 92-93, 99
Bartholomae, David, 61-62, 67
Belenky, Mary Field, 75, 82
Berlin, James, 9, 17-19, 35
Birkenstein, Cathy, 84-85, 94, 98
Bizzell, Patricia, 22, 35, 62, 67, 99
Boardman, Kathleen, 58, 68
Booth, Wayne C., 10, 95, 98
Braddock, Richard, 13, 17
Brannon, Lil, 11, 17, 62, 67

Campbell, Karlyn Kohrs, 31, 35, 103; *Man Cannot Speak for Her*, 31, 35
Chodorow, Nancy, 75, 82
Cixous, Hélène, 44-46, 47, 49, 56
Clinchy, Blyth, 75
collaboration, 6, 12, 16, 90-91
collaborative, 3, 30, 85, 90-91, 93, 94
composition teacher, 5, 8, 16, 52-56

Connors, Robert J., 7, 8, 17, 20, 35, 54, 67
Corbett, Edward P.J., 10-11, 17, 21, 35, 44, 50; *Classical Rhetoric for the Modern Student*, 10, 17, 21, 35, 50
critical pedagogy, 60-62, 64, 66
Crowley, Sharon, 5, 7, 9, 17, 53, 67
Cushman, Ellen, 80, 82

Daniell, Beth, 48, 50
de Pizan, Christine, 28, 35
dialogic, 90-91, 93
dialogism, 26
DiBernard, Barbara, 81
difference, 4, 6, 25, 34, 39, 82, 95, 97, 101-102; difference among women, 41-44, 78-80
Diotima, 20, 22-25, 35, 36
Douglas, Wallace, 6, 17

Ede, Lisa, 89-91, 93, 99
Eichhorn, Jill, 91, 98
Elbow, Peter, 57, 67, 95, 98; *Writing Without Teachers*, 57
Eliot, Charles William, 6, 7
Emerson, Ralph Waldo, 29, 30
Enos, Theresa, 8, 11, 17
experience, experience as resource for knowledge, 3, 13, 16, 25, 30, 44, 47, 48, 59, 101; experience of students, 64, 71, 73-74,

88, 94; experience and research, 78-82, 91

Farris, Sara, 91, 98
feminist research, 75-77, 78, 81
feminist rhetoric, 12, 15, 16, 20, 22, 26, 31, 39, 41, 45, 46, 47, 49, 64, 101
feminist teacher, 14, 58, 74
feminization, 7, 8, 14
feminized, 5, 6, 8, 10, 55, 56, 58, 85, 101
first-year writing, 8, 9, 54, 87
Flynn, Elizabeth A., 56, 67, 75, 78, 82
Framework for Success in Postsecondary Writing, 56
Freire, Paulo, 60-61, 67
Fuller, Margaret, 29-30, 35, 36, 46, 87, 92

Gearhart, Sally Miller, 85, 88, 94, 98
Gere, Anne Ruggles, 39, 48, 50, 91
Gibson, Michelle, 65, 67
Gilligan, Carol, 75, 82
Giroux, Henry, 61-62, 67
Glenn, Cheryl, 19, 23-28, 35, 99
Goldberger, Nancy, 75
Graff, Gerald, 7, 17, 84-85, 94, 98
Grumet, Madeleine R., 7, 17

Haraway, Donna, 5, 17
Harding, Sandra, 76
Harvard exam, 5, 6
Hayes, Karen, 91, 98
Heidegger, Martin, 95
Hernández, Adriana, 91
Holbrook, Sue Ellen, 8, 17, 18
Howe, Florence, 72-73, 82, 86

Jarratt, Susan C., 3, 17, 22-23, 35, 36, 58-59, 67, 88, 90, 91, 98

Johannesen, Richard L., 84, 98
Julian of Norwich, 20, 25-27, 35
Jung, Julie, 65, 67, 92, 93-94, 98

Kempe, Margery, 20, 25-28, 36, 38, 45
Kirsch, Gesa E., 17, 18, 51, 67, 68, 78, 82, 83, 91, 93, 98, 99
Knoblauch, C.H., 11, 17
Kolodny, Annette, 29, 30, 36
Kopelson, Karen, 66, 67

Lamb, Catherine E., 86-88, 94, 99
LeCourt, Donna, 64-65, 68, 92-93, 99
Lee, Amy, 52, 59-60, 68
Leichner, Amber Harris, 87, 99
literacy crisis, 7, 9
Lloyd-Jones, Richard, 13, 17
Logan, Shirley Wilson, 39, 50
logos, 10, 95
Lonn, Ella, 54, 68
Lorde, Audre, 39, 41, 43, 56
Lu, Min-Zhan, 50, 78, 80-81, 83
Lunsford, Andrea A., 12, 17, 35, 36, 89-91, 93, 99

Malinowitz, Harriet, 64, 68
Marinara, Martha, 65, 67
McLaren, Peter, 61
Meem, Deborah, 65, 67
Miller, Susan, 7, 8, 10-11, 17, 18, 53-56, 68, 85, 98
multigenre, 92
multivocal, 87, 90, 91, 92, 93
Murray, Donald M., 57, 68

Napoleone, Anna Rita, 65, 68
NCTE (National Council of Teachers of English), 13
North, Stephen M., 13, 17, 42

Ong, Rory, 23, 35

Index

Plato, 10, 21, 22-24, 35, 90
Pough, Gwendolyn D., 49, 50
Powers-Stubbs, Karen, 91, 98
Pratt, Minnie Bruce, 41, 43, 47, 50, 78

Quintilian, 38

Ratcliffe, Krista, 94-97, 99; rhetorical listening, 95-97
rhetorica, 12, 15
Rich, Adrienne, 40-41, 43, 50, 56, 73, 78, 102
Ritchie, Joy, 20, 28, 31-32, 35, 36, 38-39, 46, 48, 49, 50, 58, 68, 78, 81, 83, 99
Ritchie, Joy and Kate Ronald: *Available Means; An Anthology of Women's Rhetoric(s)*, 35, 36, 39, 49, 50
Rivera-Mueller, Jessica, 96
Ronald, Kate, 20, 28, 31-32, 35, 36, 38-39, 46, 48, 49, 50, 99
Royster, Jacqueline Jones, 33, 36, 39, 50, 79, 80, 83, 91

Schell, Eileen, 8, 18, 58-59, 68, 83
Schoer, Lowell, 13, 17
Sciachitano, Marian M., 91, 98
Shor, Ira, 61, 68
silence, 12, 31, 33, 38, 45, 74, 92

social location, 15, 41, 59, 64, 79, 80-81, 96
Soliday, Mary, 64, 68
Sophists, 22, 35, 36
Stanton, Elizabeth Cady, 31
student writing, 9
subjectivity, 15, 16, 49, 52, 66, 71, 73-74, 76, 81, 91, 103
Sullivan, Patricia A., 75-77, 83
Sutherland, Christine Mason, 29, 36
Swearingen, Jan, 24, 36

Tannen, Deborah, 95
Tarule, Jill, 75
Tobin, Lad, 57, 68, 69
topoi, 15, 39, 48-49
Trainor, Jennifer Seibel, 64, 68
Trinh, T. Minh-ha, 45-46, 47, 50, 60, 78, 103
Truth, Sojourner, 20-21, 31-32, 34, 36, 49, 103

Walker, Alice, 37, 40, 43, 50
Weaver, Richard M., 9, 21
Wells, Ida B., 32-34, 36
Winans, Amy E., 64, 68
Woolf, Virginia, 34, 40-41, 50, 72-73; *A Room of One's Own*, 40

Zawacki, Terry Myers, 91, 99

About the Author

Shari J. Stenberg is Associate Professor of English and the Composition Program Director at the University of Nebraska-Lincoln, where she teaches courses in writing, feminist rhetorics, and pedagogy. She is the author of *Professing and Pedagogy: Learning the Teaching of English* and her writing on pedagogy, teacher development, and feminist theory appears in journals including *College English*, *College Composition and Communication*, *Pedagogy: Critical Approaches to Teaching Literature, Language, Composition and Culture*, and *Composition Studies*.

Photograph of the author by Richard Stenberg. Used by permission.

www.ingramcontent.com/pod-product-compliance
Lightning Source LLC
Chambersburg PA
CBHW031635160426
43196CB00006B/422